TWAYNE'S WORLD AUTHORS SERIES

A Survey of the World's Literature

Sylvia E. Bowman, Indiana University

GENERAL EDITOR

FRANCE

Maxwell A. Smith, Guerry Professor of French, Emeritus
The University of Chattanooga
Visiting Professor in Modern Languages
The Florida State University

EDITOR

Roger Martin du Gard

(TWAS 42)

TWAYNE'S WORLD AUTHORS SERIES (TWAS)

The purpose of TWAS is to survey the major writers —novelists, dramatists, historians, poets, philosophers, and critics—of the nations of the world. Among the national literatures covered are those of Australia, Canada, China, Eastern Europe, France, Germany, Greece, India, Italy, Japan, Latin America, New Zealand, Poland, Russia, Scandinavia, Spain, and the African nations, as well as Hebrew, Yiddish, and Latin Classical literatures. This survey is complemented by Twayne's United States Authors Series and English Authors Series

The intent of each volume in these series is to present a critical-analytical study of the works of the writer; to include biographical and historical material that may be necessary for understanding, appreciation, and critical appraisal of the writer; and to present all material in clear, concise English—but not to vitiate the scholarly content of the work by doing so.

Roger Martin du Gard

By **CATHARINE SAVAGE**

Mary Baldwin College

Twayne Publishers, Inc. :: New York

Acknowledgments

I should like to thank Editions Gallimard in Paris for permission to quote from the works of Roger Martin du Gard in the Bibliothèque de la Pléiade edition, copyrighted by Gallimard in 1955. For the convenience of English-speaking readers, all the quotations have been given in English. The translations are my own. I am indebted to Viking Press in New York for their permission to substitute my somewhat more literal renderings for the standard English translations of the following of Martin du Gard's works, to which they hold the American copyright: *Jean Barois*, translated by Stuart Gilbert; *Vieille France (The Postman)*, translated by John Russell, and *Notes sur André Gide (Recollections of André Gide)*, translated by John Russell.

Library of Congress Catalog Number 67-30721

1468324

To Four Aunts,
Mary, Margaret, Mollie, and Flora

Preface

The first monograph on Roger Martin du Gard, by René Lalou, appeared in 1937. It took nearly another twenty years for other critics to deal at length with the fictional and dramatic work of the Nobel Prize winner of 1937 who was admired without being well known. A handful of volumes have since appeared, some with a particular thesis or concentrating on a single aspect of his work, others devoted to a comprehensive view. This volume is intended as complementary to the few studies which have been done in English. Martin du Gard died in 1958, and it is time for a reassessment which, though not definitive because his private papers are not yet available to the public, can take advantage of recent scholarship (to which I am indebted) and sharpen our view.

The present volume offers a detailed interpretative study of those works which at this date seem particularly important, and an introduction to less well-known works. I have tried to show the place of Martin du Gard in the fictional stream of twentieth century France and his relevance to a generation of novelists which followed him, for whom the novel became an instrument in the search for a viable politics and an authentic self. Of his excellence and his achievement the reader can judge as this study draws attention to his originality in representing the modern political dilemma and the ethical questions which are at the base of much of contemporary agnostic literature.

The staff of the Mary Baldwin College Library graciously assisted me in obtaining material, and I wish also to express my thanks to Mr. J. R. Jones of the University of Florida Libraries and to Mr. Harry Antrim of the University of Virginia.

CATHARINE SAVAGE

Mary Baldwin College
Staunton, Virginia

Contents

Chronology

1881 Birth at Neuilly-sur-Seine, son and grandson of lawyers and stockbrokers.

1884 Birth of his brother Marcel.

1892– Studies at the Ecole Fénelon, the lycée Condorcet, and
1897 the lycée Janson-de-Sailly. Private lessons with Mellerio at Passy.

1897 First baccalaureate.

1898 Second baccalaureate.

1898– Studies at the Sorbonne. Fails license examination.
1899

1900 Passes entrance examinations at the Ecole des Chartes, October.

1902– Military service at Rouen.
1903

1905– After further studies at the Ecole des Chartes, graduates
1906 in February with archeologist-paleographer's diploma.

1906 Marriage in February to Hélène Foucault. Four month trip in North Africa. Begins *Une Vie de saint*. Settles in Paris.

1907 Birth of his daughter Christiane in July.

1908 Abandons *Une Vie de saint*. Takes courses in psychiatry. Writes *Devenir!*, which appears in the autumn.

1909 Begins, then abandons, *Marise*. A fragment, "L'Une de nous," appears. Settles at the Verger d'Augy (Cher).

1910 Begins *Jean Barois*.

1913 *Jean Barois* published. Meets Gide, Copeau, and Schlumberger. First play, *Le Testament du Père Leleu*.

1914 *Le Père Leleu* performed. Frequents the theater. Mobilization, August 3.

1919 Demobilized in February. Works in theater. Keeps journal.

1920   Abandons theater work, drafts outline of *Les Thibault*. Leaves Le Verger d'Augy and settles at Clermont (Oise).

1922   Publication of *Le Cahier gris* (April), *Le Pénitencier* (May). First draft of *La Gonfle*. Close relations with Gide. First visit to the decades of Pontigny.

1923   *La Belle saison*.

1924– Finishes *La Gonfle*. Death of parents. Buys Le Tertre
1925   (Orne), settles there the following year.

1928   Publication of *La Consultation* (April), *La Sorellina* (May), *La Gonfle* (July). Visit to Pontigny.

1929   Publication of *La Mort du Père* and work on *L'Appareillage*. Visit to Pontigny. Marriage of his daughter.

1930   Works on *L'Appareillage*, writes *Confidence africaine*. Visit to Pontigny.

1931   Auto accident, January 1. Hospitalized with wife for two months at Le Mans. Revises outline for *Les Thibault*. First draft of *Un Taciturne*, which he writes in the spring during convalescence near Avignon, and which is produced by Louis Jouvet.

1932   Writes *Vieille France*. Visit to Pontigny.

1933   New outline for *Les Thibault*. Vacation near Marseille. Birth of grandson. *Vieille France* published.

1934   Settles at Nice. Visits Pontigny.

1935   Birth of granddaughter.

1936   Publication of *L'Eté 1914* in three volumes. Five week visit to Rome.

1937   Second visit to Rome. Works on *Epilogue*. Nobel Prize for Literature awarded in November. Visit to Stockholm.

1938   Travel in Europe. Work on *L'Epilogue*. *Le Testament du Père Leleu* at the Comédie Française.

1939   Visit to Martinique with his wife. Finishes *L'Epilogue*. Cruise in the Gulf, return to Europe in November via New York and Genoa, after three weeks in the United States. Settles in Nice.

1940   *L'Epilogue* appears. Leaves Le Tertre the day before the German troops come. Flees through France to Nice.

1941   First notes for the *Souvenirs du Colonel de Maumort*. Visit to Evian.

1942– Stays in Nice, except for short flight into the Lot when
1944　he is warned that his name is on a German list of suspects. Continues work on *Maumort*.

1945– Winters in Nice, summers at Le Tertre and in Paris.
1949

1949　Death of his wife.

1950　Film scenario from *Les Thibault*.

1951　With Gide at his death. *Notes sur André Gide* published.

1958　Dies August 22 at Le Tertre, of a heart condition. Jean Schlumberger, the author's brother Marcel, his grandson Daniel are with him. Burial at Cimiez. Papers deposited in the Bibliothèque Nationale.

CHAPTER 1

A Writer's Career

I *The Position of Martin du Gard*

ROGER MARTIN DU GARD's fictional world is at the junction of nineteenth century naturalism and psychological realism, on the one hand, and the contemporary social and political novel on the other. Taking inherited forms (the vast historical fresco of Tolstoy, the comprehensive Balzacian studies of personalities within a wide social context, the thorough studies of Flaubert and the Goncourts), he gave them a modern orientation. In *Jean Barois* and *Les Thibault*, he directed them towards specific political problems and utilized them as means of investigation, though not in the narrow sense of Zola for whom the novel was a demonstration, a tool of reform. As Barrès in earlier decades had used the psychological data afforded by fiction to develop a nationalistic, conservative political view, Martin du Gard, applying realism to contemporary social problems, maintained a nineteenth century tradition and also pointed toward subsequent contemporary development of the novel as a tool and an act. In our own generation, the failure of the novel to deal adequately with political questions is shown by the insufficiency of the committed writers and the growth of a literature of the absurd. Yet the realistic novel which, by its own inner rhetoric and values, deals with social realities, remains a preferred form. Martin du Gard is among those who have achieved most successfully the union of traditional fictional forms, of literary discipline and portrait of manners which are part of the French classical heritage, and of modern concerns for the individual in a society which is called into question.

At the origin of post-Renaissance literature lies self-expression. Although Martin du Gard wished to mirror the history and the society of his time and is known as an objective writer, he is nonetheless an artist of the self. His vocation found its impetus, he said, through the example of great writers he admired and in the desire to create something from himself and to survive. "At the beginning of my life as a writer, there is terror at the brevity of a human life, a passionate desire to protect oneself, to survive for a while." "The secret key of my life will have been the horror of oblivion and death."[1] While not speaking directly of himself in his works—unlike many of his contemporaries and in particular a writer he greatly admired, André Gide—he nevertheless poured into his novels a portrait of the artist, as well as a reflection of the times. In his sympathetic study, Claude Roy has written, "The discretion of Roger Martin du Gard, his very deliberate restraint, the horror he shows for all outburst, for putting oneself forward, are already the proof of the good quality of his attitude as a novelist. He doesn't like himself as much as the people about whom he writes. But fundamentally he never speaks of anyone but himself. On this paradox rests all his work."[2] Subjective and objective meet in *Jean Barois* and *Les Thibault*, where, as old Kama says in Malraux's *Man's Fate*, "The more they paint apples . . . the more they speak of themselves."[3]

Even the Marxist critic Georg Lukács, whose view is antithetical to that of the bourgeois world from which Martin du Gard sprung, has paid homage to the balance achieved in his work between the inner and the outer worlds—a balance which, for Lukács, is essential as a reflection of man's position in history, but which is very rare in modern European letters, oriented toward inner or ontological man. Lukács recalls Albert Camus' admiration for the density and three-dimensional quality of Martin du Gard's characters and sees this as an achievement of perspective. Stating that everything in an artist's life partakes of a historical character and moves toward some goal, he adds, "The selection and subtraction he [the artist] undertakes in response to the teleological pattern of his own life constitutes the most intimate link between a writer's subjectivity and the outside world. We observe here a dialectical leap from the profound inwardness of subjectivity to the objectivity of social and historical reality."[4] That Martin du

Gard was able to achieve an artistic expression which satisfied himself as a self-conscious artist and yet has objectivity and social relevance for the critic with anti-esthetic and anti-middle-class points of view is no mean achievement.

Literature is thus, for Martin du Gard, an extension of the self—a survival against the threats to man which he saw chiefly as biological and which a more recent generation is fond of calling metaphysical or existential. It is, moreover, as he practiced it, a social act, reflecting man in society and chronicling the movement of that society. Yet it is in no sense committed literature—*de la littérature engagée*. This is true, for him, not because an artist cannot commit himself, but because he *must* commit himself, not to a narrow, polemical view but rather to a view which will be incorporated into his creation. Buffon's dictum that "the style is the man," refined when Proust wrote that "Le style est une question, non de technique, mais de vision,"[5] is applicable to Martin du Gard's esthetic. Art reveals: it reveals a personal, often passionate view. But it is by essence committed to itself, and that writing which subordinates its conception and realization to a thesis is, for Martin du Gard, propaganda.

He wrote to Jean-Jacques Thierry in 1952, "I fear this Trojan-horse expression 'Liberty of literature.' It is ambiguous, too clever. I like even less, moreover, that of committed literature which is flagrantly hypocritical. For all literature which is worth something, whose author has a personality, is committed, even the *Fables* of La Fontaine . . . What is called today by that term is a *politically partisan* literature."[6]

If the emphasis has changed, from the 1890s when Gide talked about *manifestation*, to the 1940s and even the present day when Sartre's *littérature de situation* is a dominant esthetic, Martin du Gard's position remains that of the artist for whom art is the aim and the value; and even his most historically oriented volumes were written not to solve problems but to reflect in an autonomous work the face of an age. One remembers the sentence from Gide's preface to *L'Immoraliste* which could serve as an epigraph to Martin du Gard's esthetic: "There is no problem in art . . . of which the work of art is not the sufficient solution."

Martin du Gard said that he had put the best and most intimate part of himself into *Les Thibault* and his other works.[7] It is by them that he wanted to be known. Yet it follows from the above that we can in part know the works by knowing him: the man and his writings point to one another. The traditional method of literary history in France—*l'homme et l'œuvre*—is applicable for Martin du Gard with the reservation that nowhere is it a question of an autobiographical work.

II *The Man*

It is too early for there to be a detailed biography of Martin du Gard.[8] The facts are limited; his personal papers, including a journal kept for thirty years and a voluminous correspondence, now deposited in the Bibliothèque Nationale, will not be available until the 1980s at the earliest. Only when the majority of these are edited and published will biographers have the makings of a definitive study, which will probably render previous books obsolete. Until then, Martin du Gard remains our contemporary, a man known in public but whose inner life is not yet in the public domain.[9]

Nevertheless, from the testimony of friends and associates and from his own autobiographical *Souvenirs* (which centers around his work as a writer), we have an acquaintance with Martin du Gard which leads to an appreciation of him as a writer and as a man. He was one of the rare artists of his generation—or any—to receive the unanimous respect of his contemporaries. Few men of letters have shown such integrity, such moderation, such other admirable personal qualities as those his associates praised in him. Camus—himself known to many as a man of integrity and charity—devotes his final paragraph of the Pléiade introduction to the human qualities of Martin du Gard's fiction and the same humanity in his character—"a man of pardon and of justice, our perpetual contemporary" (I, xxxi). Emmanuel Berl wrote, "None of my friends or comrades inspired in me more complete confidence, none was more incapable than he of complacency and imposture; none loved truth more." "He had probity. . . . Without pedantry, without illusion, without ambition, without vanity."[10]

Perhaps it would seem that the character of a writer, particularly on the plane of the quotidian, is not relevant to appreciation of him. Yet in a century characterized by what Ortega y Gasset has called the dehumanization of art, personal and humane qualities may be more pertinent than we allow to any ultimate judgment on a work of art; and, in any case, the personal vision of an artist using the medium of the novel has a direct bearing on the breadth and credibility of his characters, against a background that must needs include social and moral questions. Claude Roy, writing from a Communist viewpoint, notes this moral element in the genre of the novel and in particular in Martin du Gard's fiction: "Every novel is an answer to the most difficult of questions that each one asks himself: how to behave with others, with our own family, with the world? . . . Before being a fable, a document, a pastime or a simulation of the real, a novel is a lesson in conduct. . . . In the art of the novel, every problem in esthetics is at the same time a moral problem. This is why I think that Roger Martin du Gard is one of the greatest novelists of our time."[11]

Both Martin du Gard's commitment to his vocation (his own term) and his perspective to see beyond or around it attract our admiration. In a sense, he was the perfect figure of the artist, spending all his mature life at work on plays and novels and requiring of himself that a work meet his own high standards of excellence. He was also a husband and father, a friend, an active figure in dramatic circles, and a participant in the war of 1914. He maintained cordial relations with dozens of friends and literary figures. Thus he was not a high priest of a literary cult which would replace the business of living, after the symbolist caricatures, but rather an artist writing from the point of view of a man in society. Camus observes that on the question of art as a religion, "Martin du Gard immediately separated himself from the theoreticians of art for art's sake, and symbolism . . . never had an effect on him . . ." (I, xii). The admiration which this balance aroused is reflected in the special number of the *Nouvelle Revue Française* (December, 1958) which groups the homages paid to him at his death.

III *His Youth*

His personal modesty, his retiring ways were not those of his class. He was born in 1881 into the *bourgeoisie de robe,* that world of notaries and lawyers which looks down in comfortable superiority on most other classes of French society. In the years when he was growing up, the solidity of this caste was not questioned, except by peripheral groups of socialists and anarchists. During his lifetime Martin du Gard retained in most respects the habits of living of the comfortable bourgeoisie, and his novels reflect this layer of society.[12] But his own understanding was such that he could judge his class, see its weaknesses, understand the historical pressures upon it, and explore in his fiction the possibilities for social change.

Of his childhood and rearing we know little.[13] In his novels, childhood plays a small role; the focus is much more often on adolescence. He grew up in Paris and went to a private religious school, the Ecole Fénelon, as a part-time boarder, while taking courses at the lycée Condorcet. He had little success with studies for some years. One of the revelations of his childhood, however, was the discovery that one of his schoolmates was writing plays in verse; then reading them with rapture (I, xlii-xliii). The excitement which Jacques Thibault and Daniel de Fontanin (in *Les Thibault*) feel in sharing favorite poems may well be a reflection of this enthusiasm; and the example was significant for his future development. "This need to write, which has tormented me all my life, was born, I think, on a spring evening under the charm of the dramatic works of my friend Jean." He read abundantly authors like Zola and Octave Mirbeau and started writing both verse and short stories.

He later became a boarder with a professor from Janson-de-Sailly named Louis Mellerio. Opening their library and their conversation to the boy, the professor and his wife encouraged him so that he widened his intellectual horizons immensely, acquired a taste for his studies, worked constantly and passed his examinations for the *baccalauréat*. His praise for the Mellerios is high, and we see their influence upon his youth clearly, whereas that of his family is not visible in his memoirs. One is not to infer necessarily that family relationships were unsatisfactory. They were probably not relevant to his future career as a writer. Among other debts to Mellerio which he recognizes is that of "the feeling for *composition*." He practiced by making topical outlines for countless subjects. "It was Mellerio . . . who inculcated in me this notion: that any piece of writing—

even a school composition—must have the characteristics and qualities of a construction . . . " (I, xlvii-xlviii). Martin du Gard has one of the best senses of fictional composition among writers of his generation. This early lesson helped him to handle the wide panorama of *Les Thibault* and to balance the history of a society with the study of individuals.

The abbé Hébert, director of the Ecole Fénelon, gave him to read, when he was about seventeen, *War and Peace*. Thus began his acquaintance with Tolstoy and an admiration which never ceased: one of those "elective affinities" such as writers experience, and a positive influence, the strongest of his whole career (I, xlviii, 569). This reading oriented him towards the genre of the novel and in particular the long fresco-type novel. Martin du Gard claimed later that Tolstoy's influence can be only beneficial for a young writer, for Tolstoy—to whom he paid homage in his Nobel Prize speech—has no personal technique which can be imitated, but uses simplicity and naturalness of style, presents real humanity, and teaches one to see life in depth (I, xlix).

After taking his baccalaureate degrees, Martin du Gard enrolled in the Sorbonne, then at the Ecole des Chartes (a preparatory course for historiography and paleography). His decision to enter this school was made without his parents' knowledge and as a stopgap until he could do what he really wanted—write. As a mature man, he recognized two important aspects of the influence of this training: first, the attention he was forced to pay to the past, with the result that a new curiosity for contemporary history also was aroused in him; and, second, the method of research and the sense of discipline which the course inculcated. His technique of composing his novels by means of note-cards, after a thorough documentation of the social and historical circumstances and even the composition of a dossier on each important character, is, by his own admission, a result of this influence (which, he allows, was perhaps not altogether fortunate, since documentation in or behind a novel does not always add to its real weight). His asceticism, his willingness to destroy whole chapters and books when he realized that they were not suitable, recall also the willingness of the historian to sacrifice research which is proved invalid.

As for the first influence—the sense of history and situation—it was just as lasting and, I think, a fortunate one. The scope of his novels and their sense of history are qualities which set him apart from others of his generation like Paul Morand, Jacques de Lacretelle, and Jacques Rivière, whose attention was turned more exclusively to the human heart. When he writes that "It had become impossible for me to conceive a modern character detached from his time, from the society, the history of his time," we think at once of Sartre's "literature of situation" (I, li).

At the Ecole Fénelon, Martin du Gard's chief mentor was the abbé Hébert, at whose death he wrote a tribute which appeared in 1921 and is included in the *Œuvres complètes*. He had exercised what Martin du Gard considered an entirely favorable influence since 1892 when, entering the Ecole Fénelon, he chose the priest as his confessor. Martin du Gard states explicitly that though he himself had no real sense of personal religion, no inclination to piety, he admired the priest greatly (I, 564-65, 567). Hébert's own understanding of religion was such that Martin du Gard never felt uncomfortable or hypocritical in his presence.

In 1896 Martin du Gard left the school but continued to see Hébert every month. On one of these occasions he announced that he would not take communion at Easter—a decision marking his determination to break with a doctrine in which he no longer believed (I, 569). He states that the priest discouraged him from taking this step and tried to revive his failing belief —although he himself was undergoing a similar religious crisis. After a year of dialogue, Hébert finally recognized that argument was useless; it was then that he proposed to Martin du Gard what the latter calls "the symbolist compromise" (which will play a role in the dialectic of *Jean Barois*). This, too, was the subject of endless discussions. The younger man predicted to the priest that in the long run the latter would not find this symbolic understanding of Christianity acceptable.

When Hébert published a volume entitled *Souvenirs d'Assise*, it came to the attention of the Church authorities in Paris (in circumstances which will be recalled in the episodes of Jacques' notebook) and caused him to be removed from his position at the school.[14] Martin du Gard witnessed his suffering at this time, as well as later when he was deprived completely of his sacerdotal role (I, 572). They remained friends, and the novelist attests to the strong influence which Hébert continued to exercise over him through his integrity and his spirituality. He gave one day a sort of testament which inspired the author's portrait of Luce in *Jean Barois:* "I hope to die standing, that is to say, in full lucidity. To die as I have lived, without fear of the consequences, sincere up to the threshold of—of what, I do not know—of eternal life, doubtless. For, though I do not believe in a personal God, I have not ceased believing in the immortality of my thought and of my effort towards Good . . . I wish for myself a very conscious death" (I, 575).

IV *His Maturity*

Martin du Gard took his Chartes diploma in December, 1905. When he married Hélène Foucault, daughter of a Parisian lawyer, in February, 1906, the couple left for a trip to North Africa, where he drew up the outline for his first work, to be titled *A Saint's Life.* One should note that the priest—a figure recurring frequently in his work—here was to be the central character, whom the author wanted to follow through his religious evolution and his life, to his death. He had written the equivalent of two volumes, without advancing far in the priest's life, when, reading the text to a friend, he perceived that it was not a success. The dialogues (the chief means of presentation) dragged out and he was not able to sustain the portrait. Putting this aside, he decided to take a few courses in psychiatry. At the beginning of the spring of 1908, he went with his wife and infant daughter to an inn at Barbizon and there wrote in only a few weeks the first draft of *Devenir!* After some polishing, he submitted the manuscript to Ollendorff, who consented to publish it at the author's expense. When it appeared in the autumn, it obtained a *succès d'estime* which encouraged him and whetted his appetite for beginning a new work—some major creation (unlike *Devenir!*, which he considered almost an improvisation [I, lii-liv]).

He launched into a new project, a long life history of a woman. In spite of his gifts of concise expression and his sense of classical balance and the revealing trait, there is in Martin du Gard a deep-rooted tendency toward totality—the total understanding of an individual, the complete picture of a life or of a society. "I like," he writes, "for an author to exhaust his subject, in the manner of the great Russian or English novelists" (I, cxix). Later novels would likewise be an attempt at a thorough, total vision of man and human experience. He had been reading Romain Rolland's *Jean-Christophe*, Dostoyevsky, Eliot's *Middlemarch* and *Adam Bede*, Hardy's *Tess of the D'Urbervilles*, and works by Gogol and Selma Lagerlöf—comprehensive works which impressed him as Tolstoy's did (I, liv). *Marise*, the new work, was to take a woman from birth to death, through her last revolts and her resignation. In commenting later on this project, the author noted how curious was this obsession of his, as a young writer, with decadence and death. Part-way through, he realized that the subject was not suitable for him. Abandoning it, he saved only a portion which, under the title *L'Une de nous* (suggestive of Maupassant's *Une Vie* and of Jules Romains' *Mort de quelqu'un* which would appear in 1911) was published at the author's expense by Grasset. Realizing its inadequacy, he had the edition destroyed a few years later.

With his wife's approval, he decided to live in the country and devote himself to a new work, the life story of a man. Between 1910 and 1913, at the Verger d'Augy in the Berry, he composed his first major work, *Jean Barois*. Having contracted to take Martin du Gard's next work, after publishing *L'Une de nous* at the author's expense, Grasset read the manuscript and consented to publish it, but he insisted that the form was so unwieldy that the book would be a failure. Not knowing whether to destroy the manuscript or to search elsewhere for a publisher, Martin du Gard met one day Gaston Gallimard, a friend from the lycée Condorcet, then engaged in the new publishing enterprise of the *Nouvelle Revue Française* along with Gide, Jean Schlumberger, and Jacques Copeau. Gallimard offered to show the manuscript to his colleagues. Schlumberger read it with approval and sent it to Gide, whose warm praise contrasts with his notorious judgment on *Du Côté de chez Swann*. "A publier sans hésiter," he telegraphed. When the novel appeared at the booksellers in November, Gide's judgment was vindicated in part by approving letters from Alain, Remy de Gourmont, Péguy, Suarès, and Paul Desjardins; but the journalistic reception was cool. Yet, as he soon realized, he had crossed an important threshold. Recognized as a novelist, he was also soon to become a friend of the *"équipe" NRF* and part of the Parisian literary scene.

His acquaintance with André Gide, the *éminence grise* of the review, developed fully only after the war. In 1913 he became well acquainted with Jean Schlumberger and Jacques Copeau, whose time was devoted to the newly-founded Théâtre du Vieux Colombier. He decided to spend the winter in Paris and, throughout the season, spent much time watching rehearsals and chatting with Copeau and Louis Jouvet. His own keen interest in the theater made him a fascinated observer of Copeau's new departures. Their friendship soon went beyond the bounds of interest in the theater. Martin du Gard has recounted their long evenings of conversation, when the topics ranged from their own personal lives, very different, through common acquaintances, to the esthetics of the novel. Copeau sharpened the comprehension of his friend and helped him to the awareness of his own position. "If, later, in some passages of my books, I was able to show some qualities of an observer, I am in part indebted for it to Copeau." (I, lxxv)

Without doubt this period was one of maturation and of increasing consciousness of himself as artist. "Never did I feel less worried, less morose, never did I have such natural confidence in myself and in the future as during that unforgettable winter of 1914 . . ." (I, lxxv). In February, 1914 Charles Dullin created a role in Martin du Gard's first play at the Vieux Colombier, *Le Testament du Père Leleu*. Additional works for the theater might well have followed, had not the war begun the following summer.

On August 3, Martin du Gard joined his unit, responsible for transportation of munitions and food for the First Cavalry Corps, and remained with it during the war. He began taking notes on the maneuvers and events. In 1919 this notebook was continued as a journal. From his indications, one would surmise that this diary, as yet unpublished, is less rich in speculations on art than that of Gide, less a mirror of the inner man than that of Stendhal. The contrary, however, may turn out to be the case.

Demobilized in February, 1919, Martin du Gard returned to Paris and immediately began to help reopen the Théâtre du Vieux Colombier. He had been hoping to create a new comedy of stock characters, modeled on the Commedia dell' Arte but using new figures of his own creation, taken from the contemporary world: Monsieur Punais, the adipose bourgeois; Monsieur Malandrin, the slick gangster; Falempin, his right-hand man (I, lxxix). But the necessity of working on the theater building and of assisting Copeau was more urgent than creating this new *Comédie des Tréteaux*. While his wife organized a costume studio at the theater, he assisted Copeau, along with Jean Schlumberger. During the spring of 1920, he must have experienced some difficulty in working with Copeau; for reasons which he does not explain sufficiently, he left the group and returned to his own career, as he isolated himself at the Verger d'Augy and began the outline for a major work, *Les Thibault,* of which the first idea had come to him the preceding January.

Returning to Paris with boxes of notes and a complete plan of the work, he looked for a more suitable retreat than the Berry in which to compose the long work, and found a house in Clermont, in the department of Oise, at an hour's distance from Paris, where his daughter and wife remained. He had already used this setting for the provincial scenes in *Jean Barois* and in an unfinished autobiography, of which the first chapter would appear in 1929 under the *Noizemont-les-Vierges* (I, lxxxiii). For several years he spent the weeks at Clermont and the weekends in Paris. Combining the advantages of solitude and long work-hours with the pleasures of company and the Parisian milieu at the end of the week, this rhythm suited his needs. In addition to writing, he read at length: Saint-Simon's *Mémoires* and those of Retz, Sainte-Beuve's *Lundis* and *Port-Royal,* novels of Richardson, almost all of Diderot, and long chunks of Rousseau, Michelet, and Montaigne. The classical bent here is to be noted; but even more significant is the choice of works which, with some exceptions, are either narrative or historical or comprise a vast scope.

In August, 1922, Martin du Gard participated for the first time in one of the *décades* at Pontigny, founded by Paul Desjardins, which brought together men of letters, painters, and critics for ten days of discussions. This visit was renewed nearly every summer throughout the '20s. Though he has stated that the influence of these associations was less than that of the *NRF* group some ten years earlier (or rather, to some extent duplicated it, since many of the participants were the same), he was nonetheless excited by the ambiance of the *décades* and in particular by Desjardins himself, "the most remarkable mind and the most disconcerting character I ever met" (I, lxxxviii).

The decade of the '20s was for Martin du Gard the decade of *Les Thibault*.[15] After completion of the whole plan of the novel, he published three parts in quick succession. He and Gide exchanged several visits. In 1924 he completed a play, *La Gonfle*, and, in 1926, settled at a recently-acquired property, Le Tertre, to continue *Les Thibault*, of which three more parts appeared by 1929. He began work on the following part, *L'Appareillage*, went to Pontigny in August, and married his daughter to Marcel de Coppet, whom he called, in dedicating to him *La Gonfle*, "my best friend for twenty-five years" (II, 1167).[16]

Up to this point he had followed exactly the outline he had prepared for *Les Thibault*. Such would have continued to be the case, probably, had not he and his wife had a severe automobile accident in January, 1931, and been hospitalized at Le Mans for nearly two months. Although a first draft of *L'Appareillage* was entirely composed and the first half ready for the press, he was led to an examination not only of that part but also of his intentions for the remainder of the series. In the leisure of the hospital, he criticized his plans and determined to revise the remainder. As diversion, he also drew up the scenario for *Un Taciturne*, his third dramatic piece, produced in October. Upon leaving the hospital he burned most of the manuscript of *L'Appareillage*.

It was in the postwar period that the friendship between Martin du Gard and Gide developed into a close dialogue. The association had begun as the admiration of a younger writer for one of the establishment. When Martin du Gard heard Gide read *La Symphonie pastorale* in 1919 and, for the first time, criticized him, it delighted Gide.[17] The two novelists, working on *The Counterfeiters* and *Les Thibault,* exchanged observations on the art of the novel and read to each other for criticism long extracts from their work. A voluminous correspondence was carried on for the next thirty years.[18]

This was not, however, a friendship of mere resemblances. Each appreciated in the other a mind different from his own, which, rather than mirroring his thought, could help it assert itself by contrast. Martin du Gard said of Gide, "We're scarcely ever in agreement."[19] On their common ground of a highly developed artistic sense and an insistence upon superior standards in composition, they offered distinct points of view on the novel. Gide's desire to experiment—to make *The Counterfeiters* a "vertical" novel, without a center and without a foreseen denouement—surprised Martin du Gard with his traditional sense of fictional development. Martin du Gard's advice to *compose* probably helped Gide find a balance between spontaneity of imagination and the logic of the novel. Gide tended to urge Martin du Gard to utilize additionally his imagination and not to kill the perspicacity and freshness of his views by a too-controlled language. Gide stressed that his friend belonged to the line of Tolstoy—clarity and uniform "lighting"—whereas he preferred Dostoyevsky, with his *chiaroscuro* and his element of surprise (II, 1370).

On a more personal plane, Martin du Gard, who was without priggishness, nevertheless advised Gide, in vain, against the publication of *Si le grain ne meurt* and *Corydon,* on the reasonable grounds that the resulting scandal would far outweigh their utility. Martin du Gard's essentially bourgeois position—the horror of scandal, the conservatism—is revealed here.

Commenting in 1943 on an observation by Ramon Fernandez who placed him in the "Gidian line," Martin du Gard protested, "Obviously, my close intimacy with Gide, with his person, his life, his associates, had for my interior growth a considerable importance, of which I haven't stopped harvesting the benefits. However, these advantages are of a general order. Gide's example and contact certainly raised my scale of values, increased my demands on the 'quality' of a work of art. But, on details, on the conception of the novel, on the architectural (and not symphonic) composition of the novel, on the method of working, on technique, our ways of seeing are irremediably irreconcilable" (II, 1417). He observed even, "No book by Gide has been for me one of those bedside books, on which one models himself gradually after a slow and long acquaintance. Tolstoy, yes. Chekov, Ibsen, George Eliot, yes. Others also. But not Gide. Not even his *Nourritures*, nor even his *Journal*" (II, 1418).[20]

In the spring of 1932 Martin du Gard composed the naturalistic novel, *Vieille France*. In 1933, in a hotel near Marseille, he worked on the new outline and the documentation for the continuation of *Les Thibault* and composed most of it there in the following years. In 1936 and again in 1937 he spent several weeks in Rome. The Nobel Prize was awarded him in November, 1937, and he traveled to Stockholm the following month to give his acceptance speech—the only occasion on which he spoke in public—then took an extensive trip through Europe. The *Epilogue* was begun at Le Tertre in the spring of 1938 and finished at Martinique in 1939, shortly before he and his wife took a cruise in the Caribbean and traveled in the United States.

V *After* Les Thibault

Martin du Gard spent most of the war years at Nice. From 1945 to 1949 he spent his winters in Nice and his summers at Le Tertre, with short stops in Paris. His wife died in November, 1949. The following year, with Pierre Herbart he created a film scenario from the first two volumes of *Les Thibault*. He witnessed Gide's death in 1951, admiring his gift of "dying well"; his own death came in 1958.[21]

The *Notes sur André Gide* (1951) are the only work that Martin du Gard published after the *Epilogue*. Much time during his last years was, however, devoted to a major literary project, a novel into which he hoped to pour his view of life and, in a sense, his total experience—not of course without reflection and arrangement. It was not to be autobiographic but rather the portrait of a character different from the author but through whose thoughts he could approach a variety of problems and considerations. Notes concerning the *Journal* or the *Souvenirs du Colonel de Maumort* are found in the *Œuvres complètes*, in the form of extracts from the author's journal and letters exchanged with Gide. The method with which Martin du Gard composed some of this novel, his difficulties, and his reasons for abandoning it are revealing of his esthetic.

The novel was to be the story of a retired colonel who, during the German occupation, wants to relive, through memory and in a diary, his youth. First, Martin du Gard composed the diary. Finding, however, that this was not persuasive because he was not well enough acquainted with his character, or, better said, because the character was not fully conceived, he decided that he would have to *write* in the third person the story of Maumort —a sort of first draft of Maumort—before continuing with his journal. That is, he had to portray the character with his entire biography before he could choose the details and the reflections suitable to his old age and the circumstances. This preparatory composition advanced slowly, partly because, during the early war years, the author was not in good health because of poor nourishment, partly because the project required, perhaps, a faith in the future which was difficult to muster in the early '40s. After having written for two months, he had not carried his character beyond his adolescence. Nevertheless, he persisted in the attempt, carrying out also an elaborate documentation on current events and the first months of the war so that the remarks of the colonel would be true to the situation.

The novelist recognized that another writer might not feel the need to document so extensively and to create the totality of his character's life before selecting details to go into his *Souvenirs*. The reasons he gives for continuing are illuminating. Speaking of Flaubert, he writes, "I obey (as he does) an imperious concern for *reality*. I am built so that, in order to create a character who is alive, I have to feel informed on all the facts of his public and private life. . . . In rooting him in a strict historical truth, I give to Maumort a more precise reality, a sort of concrete consistency, and, at the same time, a greater human truth. The historical accuracy of the biography which I am drawing up for him now facilitates the perfecting of his psychological truth" (I, cx).

After eight years, he had no more than a few completed chapters and a great quantity of notes. By this time, two psychological factors had intervened to make composition more and more difficult. One was imposed from without: increasing lack of confidence in the future, and realization that, after the intervening war, the world was essentially changed, and what was written on the assumptions of the pre-war world would no longer be valid. He wrote brutally that what he was imagining would have been suitable for the reader of 1910 but no longer corresponded to contemporary tastes and concerns (I, cxxxviii). "It is of the past alone that I am contemporary . . ." (I, cxxi). (One must mention also the impingement of historical concerns on Martin du Gard throughout this period. He spent hours reading the newspapers and dwelling on the events.) The other psychological factor came from within: not so much weariness as a recognition that, although what he was writing was good in conception and style, it was bringing nothing new to the domain of literature or sensibility. A less exacting author would have been content to produce another work with the same qualities found in *Les Thibault*. Martin du Gard felt increasingly, however, that a mere repetition was not justified. "What I am capable of does not warrant my wanting, at any cost, to produce more and publish . . ." (I, cxxi). Although Gide praised the fragments of Maumort, saying that his friend had written nothing better (I, cxl), Martin du Gard felt that he had already taken the measure of his ability and that he would not produce a masterpiece. It is admirable to see a writer of his age, with reputation and a solid published work, become more demanding rather than less so. In a paragraph of his journal—which interests the reader as being one of the few texts, with the Gide letters, which were not written principally for publication—he notes, "Why harness myself body and soul to this new work, since I now know the limitations I cannot go beyond . . . In order to do something worthwhile, one has to take oneself momentarily for Goethe, and believe that one is going to write *Faust*. Illusions of this sort are forbidden to me, and nothing will change that, neither the Nobel prize, nor Gide's approbations . . ." (I, cxxii). He adds that it is some satisfaction to realize that this judgment, which is neither, he thinks, self-flattering nor self-deprecating, has been his own, not imposed by the public. Lucidity was always a value for Martin du Gard, in his judgment of himself as well as in his literary works.

Increasingly he was convinced that he could not deal, nor could any writer, with contemporary history with the same perspective he had on the first decades of the century. The current scene seemed to him the province of the journalist. In a passage which shows how opposed he was in one way to Sartre's doctrine of *littérature engagée,* in spite of his focus on political and social realities, he wrote, "Those writers—and I am thinking of the best—who think they must descend into the arena and deal with current events usually do poor work. . . . Their style is degraded . . . I don't throw stones at them. . . . But one has the right to deplore it; they let themselves be blinded by an apparent 'immediate duty' . . . and neglect their real duty which, it seems, would be to pursue their writers' work" (I, cxxviii).

The last remark from his diary in the *Œuvres complètes* concerning *Maumort* is the simple reflection (1950), "All that is not so important" (I, cxlii). Without having lost his ability, he had lost his persuasion of the value of his work and his strength to pursue the arduous task of a total life-view in multiple volumes. If the other papers which deal with *Maumort* are published after 1988, one may find that the work had so much potential interest that the author's decision will seem particularly regrettable.

CHAPTER 2

The Early Works

I L'Une de nous

GAETAN PICON has asserted that Martin du Gard's first published novel, *Devenir!*, interests us not in itself but because the author is the future author of the *Thibault*.[1] This novel and the early naturalistic story which was published under the title *L'Une de nous* are in Martin du Gard's work what *Les Plaisirs et les jours* is for readers of Proust: a revelation of the author's nascent capacities and tendencies, and a first expression of what would become central themes and a fundamental vision of human life. Although the reader finds intrinsic interest in these two early works of fiction, he is likely to read them in the light of later works and to compare their shortcomings to the successful achievement of the author's novels of maturity. Since *Devenir!*, composed before the fragments entitled *L'Une de nous*, is complete, it throws more light on succeeding works and deserves lengthier commentary.

L'une de nous, not included in the complete works, contains the episodes the author salvaged from his unfinished early novel, *Marise*.[2] About a hundred pages long, the story concerns the central, and crucial, years of a young woman's life. Unlike *Devenir!*, the text was the result of lengthy planning: yet Martin du Gard could not bring his idea to a successful conclusion. The character was, in some ways, too foreign for him; his imagination was not yet ready to enter so sympathetically into the life of a woman.

Marise has married a cousin twelve years her senior to whom she was greatly attracted as an adolescent and who has chosen her because her innocence appeals to him. The marriage is unsuccessful, and Raymond continues his debauchery. They have a sickly child. One night Raymond has a stroke and is carried home. To conclude a partial, and deceptive, recovery, they have sexual relations which lead to a second stroke and also to pregnancy. Marise is horrified by the idea of another child, who may be tainted with her husband's congenital weakness. She revolts against her religious belief and against life, which has treated her unjustly. Raymond is left an invalid. She considers suicide but is terrified by death; only despair remains for her.

Both themes and characters here adumbrate scenes in the novelist's masterpieces. The marriage suggests that of Mme de Fontanin and her husband in *Les Thibault;* Marise experiences the same ambiguous recoil and attraction as that of Mme de Fontanin. Antoine Thibault and the doctor, who is here a secondary character, share a number of characteristics.[3] The chief themes are all familiar to readers of Martin du Gard: destruction, evil, and suffering; their end result, death; sexuality; and the loss of faith. Marise's life is characterized by suffering, and the rest of her existence will be poisoned by what she has experienced in these pages. She muses over the ruins around her: the end of her adolescent hopes, her idealism in marriage; her gradual transformation into an old woman. Similarly, she sees destruction in the body and the destiny of her husband. When she must witness the death of her great expectations, like Martha in Camus' *Le Malentendu,* she rebels against fate: she refuses God and encloses herself in her bitterness.

Whereas, in *Jean Barois* and especially in *Les Thibault,* the scenes of disappointment and death are both controlled and poignant, acceptable to contemporary tastes through their sobriety yet moving and full of the sense of loss, it has been observed that, in *L'Une de nous,* the portrait of Marise's bitterness, while not weak through improbabilities, is not convincing.[4] Similarly, her religious revolt, though not unmotivated, is not analyzed with the same mastery that the author will show in *Jean Barois.* Although affective adjectives abound, they cannot carry the weight that subtler observations will in Martin du Gard's later fiction. Henry James's dictum that one should not tell what his characters are like but *show* it, applies in Martin du Gard's esthetics: unless there has been a gradual depiction of the feelings of a character, with ample opportunity for us to observe his actions and his decisions and to enter into his sensibility, the tragedy of his destiny is not conveyed. Less important than this observation, however, is our realization that Martin du Gard was already struggling with themes and metaphysical questions which are fundamental to the world of the Thibaults: the existence of evil, the role of heredity, the destructiveness of disease and death, and the choice between justification or refusal of life.

II *Devenir!* 1468324

Unlike *L'Une de nous* and the unfinished, unpublished *Vie de saint*, Martin du Gard's first published fiction and first completed novel was a spontaneous work, written probably with more feeling than the other early projects, and carried to its conclusion without extensive planning or documentation (such as that he would later use in *Jean Barois*). Yet, although its style and its characters retain some of the freshness of this rapid composition and of a young man's view of the world, its conclusion is somber, and the title, *Devenir!*, is ironical. Like all of Martin du Gard's fiction, it concerns an anticipation of greatness, and demonstrates that in spite of their expectations, men are called, not to fulfillment, but to petty, disappointing, and ultimately tragic destinies.

A friend of the hero of *Devenir!*, Bernard Grosdidier, modeled on the author himself, makes the remark that "Whatever one tries, the first book is always an apprentice's work" (I, 92). This first novel, like the episodes of *L'Une de nous,* shows the author's lack of mastery and at the same time his ability. His chief character is uninteresting; the effects of satire and irony are facile. But the portrait of the hero is nonetheless skillful, for he is consistent; and the depiction of the milieux in which he moves, particularly his family and the group of friends with whom he associates in his early twenties, is remarkable for its precise characterizations, its sense of *ambiance,* its accuracy of observation. The novel is written in the traditional third-person voice, with an omniscient narrator. Martin du Gard uses both direct statement and demonstration by means of scenes and oblique suggestions; as the novel progresses, the latter predominate over the former and strengthen the impact of the narration.

André Mazarelles, who has just finished his military service, wants to embark on a literary career. As the story begins—*in medias res*—he is explaining his ambitions (the subtitle of the first part is "Vouloir!") to his family and to his friend Bernard, who (like Martin du Gard) is studying at the Ecole des Chartes. His father, a notary from the tradition-bound bourgeoisie, disapproves of his son's ambitions and wants him to study law. The family conflict which jells around the young man's ambitions is portrayed skillfully: the father and mother do not appear ridiculous, and though the novelist's sympathies go to André sufficiently to portray him, there is implicit criticism of the facile, irresponsible way in which he insists upon going to Paris to write.[5] Even Bernard crticizes the naïveté of his friend.

André dreams of creating a new kind of novel, with a variety of elements: newspaper fragments, character sketches, extracts from diaries, and so forth. One may suppose that this is a first statement of some of the author's reflections on the form of the novel, which will terminate in the dramatic and *collage* form of *Jean Barois*. The preoccupation is timely, furthermore, since it was in the early years of the century that Jacques Rivière and André Gide, among others, were proposing a break with the realistic fictional technique of the nineteenth century and the creation of a modern form. Nevertheless, the project appears in an ironic light when one realizes that André will not pursue this creative idea. In fact, he is incapable of following through on any of his literary projects.

He begins his studies in Paris, manages to get a *licence*, then decides to take courses at the Ecole du Louvre—which his father agrees upon in order to gain time. Meanwhile, he is an active member of a circle of young men, including Bernard, who meet in the best sort of camaraderie to discuss their plans and talk of writing and music. Again, Martin du Gard excels in the depiction of a milieu, that of capable young intellectuals in the Paris of 1908. The portraits are well differentiated, sympathetic, winning, yet not without irony. The sense of life that the novelist instills into the group of the *Semeur* in *Jean Barois* is already visible here. While André is spending his time going from one pursuit to another, some of his acquaintainces are making their way in their own careers. Dreading solitude, which leaves him to himself and to projects which he cannot pursue far without his imagination failing, he cultivates his friends as much as possible, yet discovers gradually that they have less time for him as they become more involved in their own careers.

In the second part, entitled "Réaliser," André continues to grapple with his literary ideas, to discard them, and to dissipate his intellectual energies. Though he now has a conception of a new historical novel, "between the novel of adventures and the study of manners"—"to make, with history, a psychological novel" (a formula which might be used for the achievement of Martin du Gard himself), he does not carry it further than contemplating an imitation of Barrès' *Les Déracinés* (I, 89) (a possible model for *Devenir!*). One important step in his life does occur—his break with his childhood religious belief and his family's norms. The theme is one which will be central in the author's subsequent fiction. (It is probably an autobiographic reflection.) Here, it is presented without the psychological exploration which will characterize the portraits of Jean Barois and Antoine Thibault; it is a *fait accompli* and occasions only one quarrel between him and his mother.

In "Réaliser," André also has his first experiences with love—casual encounters with little Parisian prostitutes, and then a short-lived affair with a Russian woman whom he meets at Fontainebleau, where he has gone to write in the solitude of his parents' country house. Like his unwritten novels, these loves are an imitation. The fact that the woman is much more passionate than he—that she seduces him, wearies him, and is finally abandoned by him because he fears involvements and complications—is a significant feature of André's moral portrait: Martin du Gard shows thereby the superficiality of his character. Perhaps one should underline also, however, his practicality in matters of love, which foreshadows that of Antoine Thibault. Following this episode, he returns to Paris and, having lost his enthusiasm for his writing, leads the life of an eligible bachelor, in the high bourgeois milieu to which his parents belong. There is more than a suggestion of the importance Martin du Gard gives to atavism as André takes up the manners of his class and gradually returns to its values also. This is a preparation for his decision, in a few months, to marry and settle down.

Before his marriage, however, he has an involvement with a girl of the upper bourgeoisie, whom he courts rather nonchalantly at first, then with increasing interest as he plays with the notion of love. He has the petty satisfaction of taking her away from a lame cousin who loves her desperately. But two obstacles arise: his father's categorical opposition, based on the arguments that her mother's reputation is unacceptable and that she has no fortune whatsoever; and André's own realization that the girl is stupid. When the two facts meet to make him look at her critically, he is able to extinguish his former interest without difficulty, since it had no real quality. During a ball, he meets the girl's cousin, who, unlike her, is ugly but also rich. Without being aware of it, André is caught by the fascination of her wealth. The part ends with a letter to Bernard in which André makes no mention of her but speaks of the appeal of a stable life, such as a friend of his has chosen, preferably in the country (she owns a large estate in the Berry), and admits that he is conscious that a literary career is not for him. Nothing has been "realized," save a discovery of some of his own limitations.

The third part, "Vivre," perceptibly shorter and with a rapidity of movement towards the unhappy ending, is concentrated around a few scenes. It is clear that Martin du Gard is already tending towards the dramatic composition which will be his principal structural technique, in which the trajectory of a hero's life is indicated by knots of scenes, between which the narrative material is minimized. André has been married to Denise Herzeaux for four years and shows in his physique the heaviness that characterizes the too-comfortable country squire. They live on Denise's property, which, since the beginning, he has had grandiose plans for improving. His neophyte's zeal for farming did not last long, but it was sufficient to involve him in expensive projects of renewal and mechanization, which he is now forced to pursue in order to try to obtain the hoped-for results. This information is indicated by a short passage of retrospective exposition; it is *shown* by a typical day in the Mazarelles' life, as André lolls around and postpones the visits he should make to various outlying lands; and Denise, pregnant, devotes herself blindly to pleasing him. The caretakers have been exploiting him from the beginning, and his debts are mounting. Yet, when the thought of his financial difficulties occurs to him, he brushes it aside and lets his present contentment possess him wholly.

The night after the opening of the hunting season, Denise becomes ill. Too late, André realizes that she is going to have her child prematurely. Only a midwife assists. The scenes of André's impatient waiting and his concern are drawn with a few, careful touches. Denise bears a girl. When the doctor arrives, he suggests that the mother be allowed to sleep undisturbed. The following day, when he and André go into her room, they find bloody sheets and discover that she has been dead for some hours. Martin du Gard uses no melodramatic comparisons here; the language is simple, and the actions speak for themselves. In more than one way, this part resembles scenes from Gide's *Immoralist* (1902). The death of the child is indicated by only a few words. A final scene—the return of his father to Paris and André's encounter with his own solitude —carries the weight of the conclusions: his youthful ambitions, his conjugal happiness, have terminated in an isolation for which he is not fitted and his bondage to a mortgaged estate. The final sentence is worthy of an heir of Flaubert: Marie, the servant girl, whose lithe body has already vaguely attracted André, "curious, leaning out of the window of Madame, watches the car which descends the avenue" (I, 203).

Except for this suggestion that he may console himself with Marie, the denouement of André's story is closed. What he had himself referred to as "the specter of failure" (I, 132) is installed definitively within his life. A weakness in this portrait, however, is that, although the reader is moved by the last passages, which indicate the loss of human life and the end of the only solid contentment which André had known, the earlier failures are scarcely moving at all; they seem insignificant, for the irony is too apparent and the reader has never been allowed to believe much in André's literary career. Thus there are two sorts of failure: the failure of a man to know himself—a major shortcoming according to the code of Martin du Gard's novels— to choose with care and to devote himself to something within his capacities (and for this, we tend to blame André for his lack of insight, his personal dishonesty); and the failure of the gods to favor human existence in its most fundamental needs of love and life. The success of the depiction of disappointment and death does not quite redeem the superficiality of the earlier character study—unlike the portrait of Emma Bovary which is meaningful throughout even though she herself is a most pedestrian human being. This is probably in part because, in the earlier chapters, André's viewpoint is subject not only to the too obvious ironies of the author's voice but to the critical scrutiny of other characters.

In later fiction, Martin du Gard will choose self-conscious characters whose sensitivity is greater, whose idealism is not self-centered, whose lives are interesting in themselves, and who have on themselves the perspective that is necessary to keep their disappointments from seeming petty and to relate their experience to a more general human destiny. This will be supported by increased technical skill. Nevertheless, it is valid to read the later fiction partly in the light which *Devenir!* throws on the author's deterministic view of man's dilemma: man who is, as the appended quotation from Montaigne observes, carried along like an object floating on the water, according to the prevailing winds.

CHAPTER 3

Jean Barois

I Composition

IN 1913, the same year that *Du Côté de chez Swann*, Alain-Fournier's *Le Grand Meaulnes*, and Apollinaire's *Alcools* appeared, Martin du Gard published his first major novel, *Jean Barois*. Its technique of presentation, classic psychological development, and timeliness make it outstanding. In spite of the political concerns, it is not merely a circumstantial novel, for the Dreyfus Affair, which fills the center of the book, is itself placed in a larger context of humanistic concern and metaphysical problems. Although the book retains the flavor of struggle, it remains principally a life history and thus has continued appeal. It was also a favorite book of the generation which was young during World War I and shortly thereafter. The admiration of Philippe Van Tieghem, who read it around 1920, is typical: he considered it a sort of bible of liberalism, read his own dramas in light of Jean's, judged his friends by their reactions to it.[1]

Jean Barois marks a crucial date in Martin du Gard's career as a novelist. It fulfills some of the aims of his early years by its contents and by a technique which is a development of the dramatic presentation he had attempted in earlier works. It corresponds to Mazarelles' aim to "write a psychological novel out of history," and its form is like one he had considered (I, 25, 89). Martin du Gard had found both the subjects and the tone which were fitting: its controlled, impersonal narration, and the political and historical element will reappear in his masterpiece.

After leaving the Ecole des Chartes, Martin du Gard had thought of making his entry into literature with a "long novel in dialogues" (I, lii, lxi). During his military service, he had composed the outline of a story, "Jean Flers," in dialogues with scene indications. He called this technique his "great idea." By his own admission he was as strongly influenced by the theater as by Tolstoy. He frequented assiduously the principal Parisian stages and knew well the texts of the popular realistic dramatists of the '90s (I, lx). When he began *Jean Barois* he was so much under the spell of the theater that he wished to create a mixed genre, sharing the characteristics of the theater as well as of the novel and having the advantages of the novelist's omnipotence in time and space as well as the dramatist's focus on crucial moments.[2] Aristotle's definition of tragedy as a presentation of an action by living actors gives, of course, the traditional understanding of drama. Martin du Gard could not achieve this live representation with such a long text. But he wished to make the same esthetic effect on the reader that the dramatist achieves through the theater: the perfect poetic illusion (such as that admired by Stendhal). Such an aim was encouraged by his strong conviction that the novelist must be unseen behind his creation. Like his contemporary Henry James, he wished for impassibility and practiced with skill the art of the disappearing narrator. "The novelist, I thought, must efface himself, disappear behind his characters . . . and endow them with a powerful enough life so that they impose on the reader a sort of *presence* . . . I had noticed, in reading modern plays, that this intensity of life . . . could almost be obtained by just reading, provided that the dialogue were perfectly natural . . . From that was born my conviction that it must be possible to conciliate the advantages of the art of fiction . . . with the privileges of dramatic art" (I, lx). The precedents of Flaubert and Maupassant come to mind. But Martin du Gard was influenced on the score of impassibility, as elsewhere, chiefly by Tolstoy and by the scientific ideal of the Ecole des Chartes.

Jean Barois, therefore, is almost entirely composed as a scenario with indications for the setting in time and place and brief descriptions of the speakers. Occasional interspersed letters and documents break the flow of dialogue. When the reader begins the book, he is struck by this scenario technique and readily imagines in his mind corresponding theatrical representations of the scenes. It is impossible, though, to sustain for long such an effort of the imagination, particularly as the situations grow in complexity. Furthermore, even with the dialogue presentation, the psychological element grows. Ultimately the poetic illusion is attained in spite of the dialogues, not because of them. Since there are no actors, the peculiarly theatrical advantages are lost. And the illusion, the sense of reality, is essentially a fictional one, not a dramatic one. It depends on word portraits and on character development; and it is stretched out over such a length of time (the fictional chronology and the time it takes to read the book) that dramatic intensity yields to a feeling of acquaintance, of *living with,* which we associate with the experience of great novels.

This is not to suggest that Martin du Gard's technique has no merits. The absence of narration forced the novelist to use, as much as possible, speech as character revelation, and to condense this character revelation into concise statements, in order to preserve verisimilitude. Under this handicap, he achieved a dense novel where each exchange in dialogue bears the weight of what would be, for another writer, character analysis. Even the shortest scenes have that weight which is characteristic of god drama. Moreover, there is a rapid pace which is suitable for the high moments of the Dreyfus Affair. In an exchange of letters with a cousin, Pierre Margaritis, in 1918, the novelist stated that the dramatic style, with the shifting focus and the abrupt changes he introduced, was one of the strengths of the book. It has the advantage of presenting characters directly, so that "one sees [them] live." "How much it is intelligently adapted to modern life . . . which is rapid, changing, cinematographic." The cinema technique is not as developed in *Jean Barois* as it will be later by André Malraux, for instance, in *Man's Fate* and *Man's Hope.* But one finds rapid scene changes as in a film, "close-ups" and distance shots, bits of characteristic dialogue. Martin du Gard rejected, however, the term "sketch" for these scenes. They are complete: as revealing as a Balzac description but by reduced, concise means.[3]

Moreover, the author achieved his aim of impersonal—though not unprejudiced—presentation. There is a particular advantage in such impersonality for a young novelist who is writing about a subject near to him in time and a character who could be an alter ego. Although *Devenir!* is less obviously autobiographic than most young-man novels, the main character in *Jean Barois* has more independent fictional reality and is never merely a mouthpiece for the direct projection of the novelist's emotional self. If Grasset was right in finding some tediousness, we can yet admire that the young writer did without narrative support so well and was able to follow a chief character and several secondary ones through presentation in dialogues.[4]

II *Themes and Structure*

Jean Barois is a young man's novel; yet, unlike Gide's *Counterfeiters,* it turns into an old man's book also. Without self-consciousness or false eloquence, the author portrays declining years and their frightening changes—foreshadowing the cruel portrait of the dying M. Thibault.[5] The novelist remarked himself on the paradox of his writing this story of human decadence while he was scarcely thirty, healthy and energetic. His systematic study of history may have developed his consciousness of human decadence. There may have been also personal experiences which gave him insight into the psychology of men and women in their old age.[6] His study of pathological cases in the hospitals may have contributed to his insight (I, lii). In any case, he shows remarkable sympathy for human feelings and a superior imagination.

In *Jean Barois* there is not just a chronological development from youth to age. The pattern is rather that of the wheel come full circle: from the feebleness and the faith of childhood through the strength and the religious skepticism of manhood, back to the debility of age with a consequent return to belief. The trajectory is both a complete and an ironic one. Its conclusion—by which no progress is made, no new value achieved —is a familiar one in Martin du Gard's world: the heroes of *Devenir!,* all the chief personages of *Les Thibault,* reach endings which are opposed to their earlier aspirations, or are at least a critical reflection upon these. The novelist had first chosen the revealing title *S'affranchir?,* and he later regretted

[44]

Jean Barois

that he had not kept it. It can be said that the theme of *Jean Barois* is the hero's powerlessness to escape the effects of his heredity and upbringing.[7]

The chronological movement by Jean's career and his evolving values are ironically illuminated by numerous elements in the book, of which one deserves note here as a major structural feature: the trajectory of his father's life in apposition to his own. The senior Barois, freethinking as his son will later be, experiences repentance and a return to piety as he approaches death, just as Jean will. Thus his career is a kind of subplot which points to the development of the main plot.

Jean Barois is one of the major political novels of the century in France, one of the first works where political concerns are raised to the level of agents and where the human dialectic is joined to the political dialectic. Martin du Gard reacted to his time with such sensitivity that he brought together, before most other writers would express this crucial relationship, the individual drama and the political drama into their real unity —into what Malraux has termed modern tragedy: politics.[8] He thus became one of the truly modern French novelists, modern in the same sense as our contemporaries like Camus, Malraux, and Günter Grass. Camus himself recognized this, noting that Martin du Gard was perhaps the only writer of his generation to announce and prepare "today's literature" (I, ix). The insights of *Jean Barois* and its artistic unity will reappear in *Les Thibault* where idealistic politics is a dramatic force and the war is a chief actor.

Like others of his generation and especially some of his elders (Anatole France, Zola, Proust) Martin du Gard saw in the Dreyfus Affair the turning point of the century and a crucial moment in the consciousness of his generation.[9] But it was after the fact that he came to this realization, for he had been too young to participate. No other novelist in France rendered so well and so artistically the complicated development of the Affair, nor made it such a major part of his work. In his study of the novel of this generation, Jean Ehrhard called it "the best novel on the moral crises of which the Affair was the center."[10] If one considers the planning and documentation which preceded the novel, one is not surprised by its accuracy and authentic quality. Martin du Gard spent ten years in acquiring and studying pertinent documents, from letters to books and newspaper clippings.[11] He poured over these as one might over the Rosetta Stone. The book was then three years in the making. The novelist was trying to achieve truth (which, according to Emmanuel Berl, was for him the pivotal question of the Affair)[12] as he had wished for truth to be discovered in the real event.

Yet, years later, he felt that the ideological element of the novel, which had required his greatest efforts, was the least successful and the least moving. Admitting that "*Barois* . . . is swollen with ideas, especially; it is an intelligent, an intellectual book . . . I do not think that a single one of the great 'problems' of the century is not at least touched on," he felt that it was small compared to *Anna Karenina*, or to *War and Peace*, which is "bathed in thought" but not a novel of ideas. The ideological element was too great, making the book "heavy and long, without genius . . ." and leaving too much in it which was perishable, unlike the human element of characterization and plot.[13] One can concur with this judgment only partially. As the author recognized, the ideas are presented with discretion; much passion surrounds them; and the Affair has relevance to the whole movement of Jean's life.[14]

If the Dreyfus Affair is at the structural and ideological center of the novel, there is also another theme which opens and closes the book and underlies the whole biographical development of the hero. This is the theme of religious belief. Again, this feature of *Jean Barois* foreshadows the central importance given in *Les Thibault* to the question of faith, where various solutions to the problem appear. Indeed, in *Les Thibault* the whole of Christian civilization seems to be on trial. With lesser scope, *Jean Barois* presents the crisis of faith in an intellectual of the early twentieth century. It is significant that the volume was dedicated to Marcel Hébert, who had by then left the Church, though retaining what Martin du Gard called his "religious sensibility." Liberalism in politics and freethinking in religion are central and are associated. But the conclusions of the novel point to the ambivalence of modern liberalism and free thought and their possible failure. Martin du Gard is a novelist rooted in his own time; but also, like his friend Gide, he speaks in a prophetic voice.

III A *Taste for Living*

Jean Barois is divided into three parts—roughly equivalent to the three ages of man. The chapter titles indicate either human growth ("The Child," "The Critical Age"), concrete objects whose symbolism is clear ("The Ring," "The Chain"), or nature. The second part is conceived as a natural evolution, centered on a storm: "The Sower," "The Foreboding Wind," "The Storm," "The Calm." Martin du Gard assumes man in a natural context, growing and developing organically, and susceptible to the changes that characterize natural life. The book ends, with an immemorial metaphor, by a chapter entitled "Twilight."

The natural context, which in Martin du Gard's fiction is also a tragic one, appears immediately in the opening scene, as Jean's father and grandmother watch over the sick boy, whose life is in danger. This first panel in the tableau of Jean's life will be balanced by the last scene, that of his death agony. Against this background appear conflicts which are fundamental in the novel. The first is faith *vs.* intellectual independence or skepticism. Jean has returned from a visit to Lourdes with his grandmother. Instead of being cured, he has grown so ill that his father, a positivist doctor, fears for his life. Yet the grandmother persists in her belief that faith is preferable to medicine. Another conflict is that of the country and the town. Mme Barois twice emphasizes the damage that Paris, with its unholy influence, did to her son and to her daughter-in-law, whose early death she attributes to the bad city air. The doctor reminds her that his wife was killed because of weak lungs, and that his son has inherited her weakness. Mme Barois refuses to recognize this hereditary element, which is crucial in Jean's life: atavism is one of Martin du Gard's major themes. During the rest of the novel, Paris will be associated with Jean's intellectual development and physical strength; his provincial home with family influences, religious faith, and physical weakness.

The absence of a mother in Jean's childhood is to be noted. In *Devenir!* Mme Mazarelles is dramatically and psychologically

uninteresting. In the Thibault family, the mother is completely
absent, and Mme de Fontanin does not give a wholly favorable
image of the influence a mother might have on her children's
lives. The adolescents in *Confidence africaine* have no mother,
nor do Thierry and Isabelle in *Un Taciturne*. Mme Barois, Sr.
here plays the mother's role—unfavorable in this context; and
she dies shortly. This near-absence of maternal figures is a
curious feature of Martin du Gard's fictional world.

Jean's father insists on the role of the will in convalescence
(as Antoine Thibault will): the desire to recover, to live out
one's life span. He alludes to the dead mother's weakness and
reveals that his marriage with her had been a union of people
who respect one another but are too different to be close. This
is a foreshadowing of Jean's marriage. The doctor's vocabulary
is significant: words like *will, energy, combat, victory* recur constantly. He makes Jean promise that he will desire to get well.
This is a victory for the naturalistic view, which places life
above all other values.

The conflict between piety and worldliness, between passive
faith and independent examination, grows when Jean, about
fifteen years old, goes to see his parish priest, Abbé Joziers, to
tell him of his doubts concerning the truth of Christianity.
Martin du Gard, who seems not to have cared for those who are
too sure of their truths, draws a portrait of the priest which is
tinged with irony, though not vicious or without sympathy.
To the adolescent's doubts the priest opposes a range of traditional arguments couched in modern terminology. Science, instead of being an opponent of faith, merely shows how
magnificent is the divine plan. When Jean raises the objection
of evil, the priest attempts to deal with the problem of theodicy
by a variety of arguments, some of which are self-contradictory.[15]
Thus: "In the first place, God did not create the world such as
it is. Man, by his disobedience to the first order of the Creator,
is responsible for what we suffer since" (I, 222). Then: "The
suffering of every creature is *willed* by God, my child, as a
condition, as the very condition of life . . ." (I, 223). He ends
by an appeal to action: the believer must reflect less and act
more. In a way, Jean will heed this observation, for the middle
part of his life will be devoted to acting out the imperatives of

liberalism. After the discussion his position remains uncertain, and he takes communion with his godmother, Mme Pasquelin, and her daughter, Cécile, who will later become his wife. The sacrament foreshadows the marriage scene later.

In the following chapter, entitled "The Symbolist Compromise," Jean is in Paris, feeling the influence of its intellectual life and of the scientific discipline of medical school and his courses in natural science. A letter to Abbé Joziers reveals his continuing search for the answer to the contradictions between science and faith. He alludes to his pure, ideal love for Cécile; the aspiration toward purity is profound in him. There follows a series of dialogues between Jean and Abbé Schertz, a Swiss scientist who is a sort of Catholic *vicaire savoyard*. Having just discovered historical scholarship, Jean raises the questions of the contradictions between dogma and history, between the Christ of the Church and the historical Christ. The conversations place us in the nineteenth century ambience in which history and faith confronted one another for the first time. And the solutions which Schertz proposes to Jean are Renanian as well as recalling the position of Marcel Hébert.

He distinguishes first between appearances and reality, between historical authenticity and spiritual truth. Using these distinctions, and placing himself in a historical perspective, he tells Jean that there are two sides to religious life: the religious sentiment which is universal and unchangeable, and the dogmatic form which the sentiment takes on. He believes in the first and in the God it reveals; he takes the second to be variable and relative. Christ is a particularly favored representative of spiritual truth and God. This solution, which sees an immutable truth behind varying appearances, is typical of late nineteenth century Christian humanism.

In a revealing outburst, Jean tells Schertz that his anguish is so great because he needs religion, even though his intellect cannot adhere to it. This perception of his own need prepares for the religious enthusiasm with which he will later give himself to the cause of Dreyfus, and for his ultimate return to religious faith. Jean wishes for a creed which will satisfy both his reason and his sensibility. If, at the end of the chapter, he seems to have resolved the question, it is because he has put it aside and because his scientific studies, currently demanding his whole adherence, have become a new creed for him, as they will be for Antoine Thibault.

The two following chapters form an ironic diptych which reveals Martin du Gard's conception of what marriage can be. In "The Ring," the engagement between Jean and Cécile is sealed at the bedside of the elder Barois, who is gravely ill. Martin du Gard's sense of the irony of destiny and the conflict between life and death is indicated by his placing the betrothal in a setting of death: life will continue from the debris of an elder generation. Jean's father shows a momentary awareness of this and feels the resentment of the dying for those who survive. At the same time, the reader learns that the father has returned to the faith of his childhood.

Father Schertz writes to Jean that he should not inform his fiancée about his religious doubts. For, even if each partner has a different way of conceiving religious truth, still the religious sentiment is fundamentally one, and differences of form are incidental. With their common background, the differences between them will diminish. Their union has been sealed by the communion they took together (a second rite between them) at his father's bedside. This advice—certainly unsound if we judge according to its results—may be a reflection of an authorial view that celibates do not understand marriage. The elder Barois comes closer to perception of things as they are when he observes that "women are different." Throughout all of Martin du Gard's fiction, woman appears as essentially *different*—unknowable, dangerous, though not necessarily the splendid animal of Baudelaire, or the sadistic, fugitive creature of Proust, or the romantic ideal. She whose social and biological destiny is interwoven with man's yet remains a stranger; there are no marriages of true minds in Martin du Gard.

"The Chain" reveals the dilemma which marriage has posed for Jean. Both religious ties and marriage—here joined in the person of Cécile—are a bond. He explains to Schertz that he can no longer accept the symbolist or metaphoric interpretation of Christian dogma, and he points out that the Church has formally condemned this interpretation. A paragraph explaining the three stages in the evolution of his religious life recalls the author's experience (I, 262).[16] He quarrels bitterly with Cécile concerning a novena she is making.

His disbelief and his failing marriage then become the subject of a quarrel with Joziers. This scene contains an admirable stylistic contrast between the heated argument and a natural setting. In a passage worthy of the Flaubert of *Un Cœur simple,* Martin du Gard writes,

> The shadows grow longer, oblique. Through the leafless tufts of the elms, through the poplars like a curtain, shine white façades, blue roofs. Almost no one. A cart proceeds on a path which he doesn't see, and the wheels grind in the mud of the ruts. In the distance, a gray horse and a reddish one pull the plow on the soft curves of the vales and raise noiselessly clouds of brown dust. . . . Deserted nests make knots in the skein of the branches. The plowers have reached the end of their field; with slow gestures, they turn around and start again . . . The wind has fallen. The bumping of the cart has ceased. Dead leaves repose. Silence. (I, 283)

This is, of course, a violation of strict dramatic technique (as are other passages which give either description of a character or the account of his thoughts). By this time, however, the reader is accustomed to the combination of dramatic scenes and intervening commentary.

The first step in "The Break" is taken when the director of a religious school at which Jean has been teaching attends a class, disapproves of the agnostic-scientific point of view, and demands that he modify it or resign. This incident recalls Hébert's departure from the Ecole Fénelon. His decision to resign precipitates a domestic crisis. Several quarrels with Cécile, now pregnant, punctuate the chapter. One might charge the novelist with needless repetition. Yet since with his scenic technique he has limited himself chiefly to showing rather than telling, only reiteration makes the conjugal estrangement appear radical.

Cécile's mother leads her to force the issue. Jean refuses her demands and instead goes to London to participate in a congress on free thought. When she gives birth to a daughter, he returns, but when quarreling resumes concerning the child's baptism, he leaves and goes alone to Paris to devote himself entirely to science and the battle against religion. In his mouth there is a taste of freedom, of a new life.

IV *The Possibilities of Politics*

The second part of *Jean Barois* invites the same criticism which has been leveled at *L'Eté 1914:* in the two works, history invades the story, bursts its boundaries (set heretofore for the individual or family), and becomes the chief drama.[17] To those who prefer the novel of psychological analysis, there can perhaps be no justification for the hybrid of individual story and collective history. One thinks, however, of such masterpieces as *L'Education sentimentale* and *War and Peace*, which show that politics is pertinent to the individual destiny. This insight —which after its aristocratic form in the *raison d'état* dramas of Corneille and Racine appears on a more generalized scale in the nineteenth century (Stendhal and Balzac have a keen sense of it)—is nevertheless chiefly of the twentieth century, where it is a fundamental datum. It was becoming increasingly clear that the fruits of nineteenth century reform would be bitter and dreadful; that political and military conflict was a moral feature of man, as Barbara Tuchman shows in *The Proud Tower*,[18] and not just a defect in social organization. Martin du Gard's perception of this places him halfway between Stendhal and Flaubert, who could deplore the tyranny of events over the human person, and Sartre, who, a century later, finds in them human possibility. Jean Barois grows and develops through political action; yet this action may not be open-ended and all the meaning of Jean's life cannot be identified with it, for he will also have his private pathetic trajectory. There are a natural dimension and a metaphysical one which the historical involvement cannot include.

Martin du Gard sees political ideologies as psychological, sociological, and, in a sense, autonomous forces. If he does not yet make ideology a structural feature of the novel,[19] he is still highly perceptive in giving it a dramatic force, and in seeing that politics is no longer a question of might of arms only but a question of the strength of the idea, liberating or destructive. His depiction of the Dreyfus Affair is more enlightening than a simple historical summary, since, without giving each step in the intricate development, it explores more fully the moral and psychological factors and gives emotionally charged views from a number of angles. As critics have often pointed out, the novelist has an advantage over the historian when, in dealing with the past, he can choose a narrow, but illuminating personal viewpoint—a single vantage point which gives a passionate insight into what an event meant to those who were living it.[20]

It need scarcely be reiterated what profound as well as immediate effects the quarrel and judicial processes concerning Captain Dreyfus had on French society and on the course of the Third Republic.[21] Historians have summarized it variously: reaction *vs.* liberalism; militarism *vs.* distrust of the army; right *vs.* left or monarchy *vs.* the republic; the church *vs.* the lay state; and, of course (using Zola's capitals), Injustice *vs.* Justice. Partisans of all these views and ideals waved their colors in the course of the battle and made the Affair into a test case for their predictions on the future of France. Personal hobbyhorses and manias, notably anti-Semitism, also played their role. In its ramifications the case touched on almost all aspects of organized social and political life, ultimately forcing nearly everyone to relate himself to it. The cleavage thus caused in the five years from Dreyfus' first trial and degradation (1894) to his retrial at Rennes, his sentence, and his pardon (1899) operated in multiple directions through all of society. If, with his final acquittal in 1906, it was Justice which won, it was also the Republic which emerged victorious over the pro-monarchist parties, lay education in particular over its Catholic opponents, change over the traditionalism of Albert de Mun and other conservative Catholics, and the Radical party—exponent of these positions—over more middle-of-the-road moderates. The generals, wishing to preserve the honor and the integrity of the army, and in many cases (though not all) of conservative political and religious traditions within it, had been willing to sacrifice much—the comfort of a captain, their own smaller honesty, the republican cornerstone of justice. Others, determined to salvage these values at any cost, fought in such a determined way that the army and its consolidated traditionalist bloc were forced to yield—and the emerging forces were all anti-traditionalist.

Martin du Gard's maturity as a novelist is indicated by the balance between the hero's own potential and the requirements of the event which the author draws him into. In earlier works the characters were not conceived and portrayed strongly enough to sustain the burden of exemplary material that they were supposed to carry. Since he had to fight against the Church so long, Jean is anticlerical as well as being an unbeliever. He is optimistic enough concerning man's future in the new society of science and enlightenment to be willing to struggle for this society; and he is full of energy and that need for a belief which he had discerned in himself. Moreover, without family life now, he is free to devote himself to a cause. Just as *disponible* as Proust's Jean Santeuil, who also becomes involved in the Affair, he is more serious and active.

Before the condemnation of Captain Dreyfus is anything but a minor incident, Jean becomes a public figure as the editor of a small review, *Le Semeur*. His collaborators share his central conviction of the bankruptcy of Christianity. But their personalities run through a wide range: from the aggressive, intransigent Breil-Zoeger to Cresteil, a revolutionary temperament with his mind fixed on eschatology, a *croyant manqué*, through Roll, who is a workingman (a typesetter, from which trade radicals frequently came), through the little Jew Woldsmuth who has a noble heart but who knows atavistically and fears so much the force of anti-Semitism that he is not easily persuaded that evil can be put down. Their discussions recall the group scenes in *Devenir!*. Martin du Gard excels at rendering this kind of intellectual comradeship based on common concerns—the kind which was important in his own life. The example of Péguy and the *Cahiers de la quinzaine* is probably not without relevance to the conception of *Le Semeur*.

To point up the significance of *Le Semeur*, Martin du Gard adds as an iconographical symbol Michelangelo's *Slave* in Jean's bedroom—the piece which Hébert had on his mantle. Socialist ideas play a considerable role in the thought of the group. They are of the Blanquist, Proudhonian, and Saint-Simonian variety, rather than the Marxist, with pacifist and idealist coloration. In *L'Eté 1914*, socialism will play a major role, with a marked conflict between the humanistic French tradition and

partisan views, the vain insistence of Zola's lawyer Labori that
the question of Dreyfus be brought out in the open, the gran-
diloquence of the generals—brings the reader face to face with
the issues and emotions as experienced by contemporaries. Martin du Gard has accomplished here a superior piece of *reportage*.
The authorial voice is at a minimum, and the focus moves in
the journalistic manner from one side to another.

In spite of the presentation of all points of view, when the
attention is on Jean and the *Semeur* we are still reminded that
this is a personal drama as well as a historical one and that the
author of necessity has a viewpoint which is expressed through
his characters and their interplay, whether directly or, as in this
case, obliquely. The reader distinguishes upon reflection that
the representatives of the military are, by careful quotation and
juxtaposition, made to look ridiculous, whereas the fire-eating
Labori is appealing and impressive. This is an example of Martin du Gard's brand of objectivity (often like the "objectivity"
of the historian which, with apparent fairness to all views,
nevertheless loads the dice in such a way that the reader's
sympathy is inevitably drawn to one figure rather than another
and the author's own sympathies—ideological and human—are
revealed).[26]

A year later, when the retrial of Dreyfus, made necessary by
the suicide of Major Henry, opens at Rennes, Jean is confident
that the end of the Affair will inaugurate a new era of freedom
and justice. Instead, Dreyfus is not exonerated, only pardoned.
In a sketch of the *Semeur* group returning to Paris after the
disappointing verdict, the novelist gives a cross-section of opinion and suggests the fatigue and deceleration of the participants
—the unsatisfactory status quo after an impassioned battle. Then
in a skillful juxtaposition which fixes our sense of failure, he
makes Jean discover, the same night, that his mistress Julia
(Woldsmuth's niece) has left him for his friend Breil-Zoegler.
Failure in love and politics are associated, as idealism in love
and politics will be for Jacques in *L'Eté 1914*. Luce presents
a summary of the battle and of the only kind of real victory
that may come of it: "The strict duty of every generation is
to go as far as it can in the direction of truth, to the extreme
limit of what it can glimpse, and to hold on there desperately,

as if it were reaching absolute truth. The progress of man is paid for by this" (I, 438). These words, which foreshadow some of Antoine Thibault's ideas, express what one can judge to be a firm conviction of the author's. Justice and truth are relative; each generation, as each individual, has the duty to find its own, as a step always toward a greater truth.

"The Calm" opens "several years later." At the Trocadéro, a great crowd of sympathizers has come to hear Jean lecture on "The Future of Disbelief." He notes the religious crisis of their era, stressing the failure of the Church to deal adequately with the problem of evil. One of the author's favorite themes, theodicy, thus returns. He affirms that religion will be replaced by a new human rallying, based on scientific knowledge and social solidarity. His program is neither socialist, Marxist, nor utopian, but only generally humanitarian and secular. The speech, which ends on a note of optimism, becomes ironic when it is juxtaposed with his subsequent reconversion.

It is another patent irony that, following this militant appeal for free thought, with its allusion to the "indelible imprint" of a Christian education, Jean, in a moment of fear when his cab collides with two trolleys, should stammer the beginning of a prayer: "Hail Mary, full of grace . . ." Later, dismayed at the force of his childhood training and at the prospect of lapsing back again as an old man, he resolves to write a profession of faith, disclaiming all religious belief, affirming his deterministic creed, and expressing a hope in science.

V The Wheel Comes Full Circle

The title of "The Crack," which opens five years laters, is an allusion both to a disappointment and a breach in the political ideal of those who had fought for Dreyfus, and a crack in Jean's interior life. He is sick, and Le Semeur has been losing subscribers. His meditation on life is paradigmatic of the whole novel: "For a long time, one thinks that life is a straight line, whose two ends plunge out of sight over the edge of the horizon: and then, little by little, one discovers that the line is cut, that it is curving, that the two ends approach, join . . . One is going to become an old man who knows only how to turn in his circle!" (I, 464). His friend Cresteil, in a diatribe which fore-tells Jacques Thibault's socialist stand, attacks the general failure of liberal politics, the disappointments of the Affair, and the utilization of principles to cover the crudest kinds of political interest.

When Barois' daughter Marie comes to spend her eighteenth year with him, he learns that she wants to join a religious order and that she is with him to test her belief. Discovering that none of his writings against religion can affect her, she is ready to return and take the veil. He sees that her faith is not of the intellectual order at all and is proof against all reasoning. A letter to Luce, after this conversation, shows how he has been shaken and how he questions the power of education ever to pierce religious belief. Moreover, gradually Jean's own intran-sigent position is eroded, as sickness gnaws at him and he again sees his wife and daughter. When Cécile finally learns of Marie's religious vocation and cannot help, as a mother, regretting it, she and Jean find a common ground again.[27]

At this "Critical Age," Jean finds himself criticizing those who do not see any good in religion and defending, as Schertz had done, not its forms but the religious feeling ingrained in man. One of his intellectual weaknesses is to judge too much in func-tion of himself. With his illness, a new thoughtfulness has arisen in him, and he cannot understand why others do not share it. He grants an interview to two young men who have answered a recent poll of his on the position of the rising gen-eration. (One thinks of the *enquêtes* such as that conducted by Henri Massis and Alfred de Tarde under the pen name of Agathon.[28]) To his discomfiture, he realizes that these students, of the highest mental caliber, reject virtually all of what the elder generation fought for: the liberalization of politics, the humanization of society, the protection of the individual. In-stead of admiring those who fought for Dreyfus, they dismiss them as opportunists. While claiming to defend republican principles, they condemn the lay state and the emphasis on a scientific basis for progress. In a word, they are the new reac-tionaries, criticizing "the stupid nineteenth century" and de-manding a return to values like Catholic discipline and morality and nationalism. Jean realizes that this is the inevitable wave of reaction after the failure of his own generation to realize the promises of the battle for Dreyfus.

Martin du Gard has accurately portrayed here a political phenomenon of prime importance in the first decade of the century, a result in part of political scares at home and abroad: the failure of the Marchand expedition at Fachoda in 1898, the German show of force in Morocco, the revolts and wars in Russia and Japan which progressively mobilized the European mentality for war and, with the old cry of revenge for Alsace-Lorraine, raised a strong war party in France. Charles Maurras' classical nationalism, based on an appeal for return to what he considered the pure or Latin genius of France, is reflected in the belief of the young men in a classical France. The nostalgia for faith of which the students speak is another characteristic of the generation before the war. One thinks of the conversions of a number of important young figures—Claudel, Péguy, and Maurras and Psichari, for whom Catholicism was of more moral and political importance than theological. This was part of a change in political climate which would ultimately bring many of the former radicals into the nationalist camp and the *union sacrée* in 1914.

Doubts concerning his own strength and judgment, doubts on the validity of his aims make Jean tender his resignation as editor of *Le Semeur*. The metaphysical dilemma of life ("a life whose meaning escapes me"), which once seemed to him a false problem, now seems very real. He rebels against the necessity of age, change, annihilation. An almost existentialist anguish bursts out as he protests, "Why are we conscious, if it is to contemplate nothingness?" (I, 523).

Fulfillment of Jean's early prediction that he has a fundamental need of religion comes in the final chapter, "Twilight," as he re-accepts Christianity, in his family home, where the elder Barois had taken the sacraments. A new character gives a view of Jean's conversion which he would himself be incapable of furnishing. Abbé Lévys, himself gnawed by doubt under the influence of scientific ideas, becomes the confidant of Jean and finds himself in the ironic position of having to forget his own hesitations and affirm to Jean the promises of the Church, par-

ticularly that of immortality. Jean is much less concerned with
the redemption of the world than with the concrete promise
of immortality (an emphasis which, as Paul Tillich points out
in *The Courage to Be,* comes chiefly from the nineteenth century rather than from older tradition). To Luce, the conversion seems purely an act of sensibility in a mind where the light
is extinguished. Luce notes that it is easier to change one's
intellectual view of the world, as Jean did, than to forget the
moral conscience and its traditional expressions which generations of mystics have developed in us. He gives an eloquent
self-apology for the man who lives without faith but who is
certain that right will triumph over wrong, who prefers this
truth to any other consolation.

Luce's subsequent death strikes the reader as being a fitting
end for his life—the kind of *mort consciente* of which Camus
spoke and which Marcel Hébert had wished. In spite of his
suffering, he remains calm, able to accept his physical evolution as a part of nature (more easily than Antoine Thibault),
and he retains confidence in his own humanism. This death is
opposed to that of Barois in the following chapter. He expires
in the midst of delirium, frantically crying for pardon and seeing
a dreadful vision of hell. Although Martin du Gard's customary
sobriety of style deserts him here slightly when he speaks of
"the *summum* of human suffering," he does finish the portrait
rapidly.

Barois' oscillating and centerless life is crowned in his death
by a final irony. Cécile finds and burns—after showing it to the
priest—the testament which Jean had written in his forties, ab-
juring all faith and stating that any subsequent conversion will
be only the effect of mental and physical debility. This statement and his final move to religion stand in continual tension,
neither one allowing us to accept the other—as though man's
reality can be located nowhere in him and must everywhere be
subject to ironic qualification. From the scientific viewpoint
which Jean had espoused, this would be the result of universal
determinism, which subjects us to physical and psychological
laws that can be summed up as flux. To a contemporary existentialist rebel, it is the hand of a cruel fate, almost personified,
which plays with men's lives and takes away their meaning.

Martin du Gard's own position was doubtless that of a naturalist: seeing lives undone inevitably by the laws of nature which condemn men to destruction. The last sentence, "A clear flame lights the room," recalls ironically the light of Luce and the light which Barois had tried to be, and qualifies his entire career as a flame which burns out.

VI *Christianity in* Jean Barois

On the question of religious belief, the weight of the evidence in the novel is in favor of rationalism rather than Christianity. The novelist does not explicitly take a stand and retains a journalistic quasi-objectivity in reporting both sides of the question, showing faith and its works beside free thought. But the silent novelist loads the dice in such a way that, fictionally, our preference has to go to Luce rather than to Joziers, to Jean rather than to Cécile, and to the serene death of Luce. The priest's action of burning the testament seems reprehensible in view of what that testament asserted. Jean's return to religion is a choice made in sickness, and under the atavistic influence which the book brings out. Marie is an attractive figure, but her choice is nevertheless condemned by the preponderance of scientific views. Arguments by the priests are refuted at least as successfully as they are presented—usually more so. In short, the principal values around which the novel revolves are those of skepticism, examination, and rationalism. One could argue that by Jean's return to belief Martin du Gard has given the final word to the Church. But, in the context of the entire novel, this final word is ironic. Even if free thought is not glorified here, certainly the ironies of Jean's evolution are a qualification to any possible religious statement.

Catholic commentators have seen this, of course. What is not agreed upon is the value to be given to this essentially critical work. It is clear that the form of Jean's skepticism represents the personal opinion of the author. Réjean Robidoux, who has studied in detail texts from Martin du Gard's young manhood, including letters exchanged by him and Hébert, points out the parallels and insists that by his twentieth year Martin du Gard had a similar non-Christian view, although not so free of a religious coloration as he later remembered. He wrote to

Hébert in 1910, "There are only two states for men, the state of faith and the state of incredulity. . . . I was certainly born *incredulous*, for I have always had a great deal of difficulty believing, have never found any real satisfaction in it, and feel that I am alive only since my definitive liberation . . ."[29] A later appraisal states that "I have never had the least religious emotion; I have as it were *no religious sentiment*" (words which will recur in Antoine's discussions with Abbé Vécard).[30]

Charles Moeller, however, feels that Martin du Gard could not be a fair judge of Christianity since the Church in France was not representative of the best in Catholicism, and that his judgments, which amount to a caricature, should be considered only contingent, not even true to what he might have thought in other circumstances. This is probably not rendering Martin du Gard a service. Moeller's apology, which blames the atmosphere of rationalism and pietism and other heresies of the time, would be more pertinent to a criticism of the forms of Christianity rather than of its essence. It is probably true to Martin du Gard's intentions to credit fully the rhetoric of the novel which brings to bear its criticism on Christian belief.[31]

Drafts for prefaces which Martin du Gard wrote but never published with the text confirm this view. In each of these, which number over a dozen and date from 1910-13, the writer, overly conscientious about the effect of his novel, warns that it is critical of religion and can inspire doubt, and that only those whose interior experience has already led them to question the tenets of the Church should read it. This is both a confession of its negative import and a disclaimer, sincere no doubt, of any intent to proselytize on behalf of science. In fact, more than the book itself, these prefaces suggest that the disbelief with which *Jean Barois* deals was a personal position which the author had experienced keenly and could not help putting into his novel, without wanting to communicate it to others who had not had the same doubts. "It is for those who suffer from the terrible contemporary conflict between a latent mystical heredity and a scientific education which is irreconcilable with it that I have wished deliberately to write this book."[32] (One can note in passing that this attitude helps us to distinguish between Martin du Gard the author, who, as he said, "tried to present, in an impartial light, the psychological curve of a soul . . ." without defending a particular view, and the authorial voice within the book which visibly leans in its sympathies towards Jean's scientific position. Of course the latter ultimately refers us back to the real feelings of Martin du Gard, the man.) "May those who fear the contact of doubt not venture into these pages." It is "poison" and "partial." "I realized this when the book was finished . . . There are burning subjects where impartiality is beyond human capacities."[33]

CHAPTER 4

Les Thibault: Le Cahier Gris
and Le Pénitencier

I Conception of Les Thibault

THE cornerstone idea of *Les Thibault*—the eight-part novel
which by its scope, its precision, and its intense impression
of life stands as a modern masterpiece—came to the author in
January, 1920. He notes in his *Souvenirs* that he was "suddenly
attracted by the idea of writing the story of two brothers: two
beings of temperaments as different and diverging as possible,
but deeply marked by the hidden similarities which a powerful
common heredity creates between two of the same blood" (I,
lxxx). (This recalls the two dissimilar friends in *Devenir!*) Such
a subject had the obvious advantages of reflection from one
hero to the other (which he does not comment on) and of
offering him the chance to express two contradictory impulses
of his nature, that toward order and measure, and that toward
independence and revolt. Just as in Baudelaire's intimate jour-
nals and Gide's fiction, there is here a many-dimensioned portrait of the artist, with contrary views coexisting and, to an
extent, criticizing each other. Oscillation (not hesitation) between the two temperaments and the views which they dictate
is a fundamental structural feature of the novel.

The idea matured in his mind during the winter, and in the
spring he drew up the complete plan of the novel. Certain
questions of technique and orientation had been solved, even
before the subject was created. In his exchange of letters with
Pierre Margaritis in 1918, he had revealed an intensive self-
examination with respect to his artistic principles and his aims.
It is significant that *Les Thibault* is dedicated to the memory
of Margaritis. After debating questions of both form and con-

tent, he had made several decisions which were carried out in the composition of *Les Thibault*. One of these concerned the role of ideas in his fiction, as opposed to characters, emotions, and sensations. He wrote, "I feel myself attracted (and the war only encourages me in this way) towards ideological works, the book with a thesis, philosophical, sociological . . . tempted to stuff my literary work . . . with ideological speculation. I am preoccupied, and am proud of it, by all the great contemporary problems, and I continue building up my documentation in this direction."[1] Nevertheless, he felt that his most characteristic talents lay not in this direction but in the portrait of individuals, the indication of emotion, the feeling of life. Even in *Jean Barois*, he preferred, to the discussions of ideas, the depiction of characters. Granted that he had ability to deal with abstract thought, too much of this would neutralize more personal (and, one might add, more strictly literary) qualities.

After continued debate, with himself and with Margaritis, during which he felt that he had to choose between two very different types of fiction, he seemed to choose to cultivate in himself the qualities of observation and notation which would enable him to recreate reality and draw living beings, and to neglect somewhat the *chartiste*, the thinker, who wanted to examine and philosophize. Thus, he concluded to Margaritis, "the novel which I am planning, this colossal novel of which I've already given you the title, *Good and Evil*, I see it as a pure novel . . . a swarming of living beings, as attractive as the very spectacle of life" (p. 1132). He decided to put into his next book only those elements of thought which would be personal. Whether this resolution was indeed carried out in *Les Thibault* can be decided after examination of the latter parts in particular. There is no doubt, in any case, that, even if there was an intermediate unfinished text, *Les Thibault* corresponds to this masterwork which Martin to Gard had been incubating: with its wide cast of characters, its concern for portraits of individuals and the illusion of real human lives, and its moral concerns expressed by the original title of *Good and Evil* (a polarity which is constantly present in the finished work).

Another question which was resolved prior to the composition of *Les Thibault* was that of narrative form. After having written *Jean Barois* in dialogues, and reconsidered it some years later as a successful experiment, he naturally considered using the same technique for his new work. To decide between it and traditional third-person narration, he composed two versions of an episode, showing the two procedures (I, lxi). The dialogue version was, he discovered, more strikingly lifelike; but in order to achieve that presentation, he had had to use so many tricks (avoiding direct narration) that the result was also long and unwieldy, compared to the version in traditional presentation. In the interests of concision, density, and *vraisemblance,* he chose then traditional narration for *Les Thibault.* He also secured, by this choice, the stylistic advantages offered by the range of past tenses, which could be used in only a limited way in the dialogue presentation. When one considers the length and the complexity of the total achievement, one applauds this choice. It remains true that many of the best parts of the novel are those where conversation carries the exposition, advances the action, and reveals character.

Armed with Gide's approval of the project, Martin du Gard cloistered himself at Clermont in May, 1920 and drew up, in considerable detail, the plan of *Les Thibault,* imagining virtually all of the characters; composing for each a life history, with notes and documentation for their evolution; and sketching out some of the principal scenes. From these notes—which filled a dozen or so folders—*Les Thibault* took shape in the following two decades. André Maurois is one of those who tell of seeing the tremendous collection of *fiches* or notes which the novelist kept on his characters.[2] With no direct reflection of the author's current life—since, except for the epilogue, the action takes place before the European war of 1914—it nevertheless *was,* in a very real sense, his life. Through his dedication to this task, he was able to make the portraits and the destiny of his characters as real for the reader as for himself.

II *Structure and Characteristics of* Les Thibault

This long *roman-fleuve* is divided into eight parts, counting the *Epilogue* which composes an entire volume. Though some of the early parts are longer than others, there is a rough symmetry between the volumes until the seventh part, *L'Eté 1914,* which in the Pléiade edition occupies 700 pages. It has been asserted that this lengthy section, which covers an elapsed time of one month and thirteen days, creates disequilibrium in the structure of the whole work.[3] This problem can be treated later. It should be noted, in any case, that the time concentration varies from volume to volume, and that a hundred pages to recount only a few days is no more exceptional for Martin du Gard than for Proust. In the first part, the action lasts only a few days; in part IV, only a day. During other volumes the action stretches over several months. There are intervals or *entr'actes* between the volumes, in which the action has proceeded, and there have been developments which give rise to the new situation in the following volume. Suspense is held, and it happens even that a crucial episode occurs before the explanation of it, so that one experiences both surprise and curiosity.

Percy Lubbock's distinction (after Henry James) between dramatic and pictorial presentations in fiction is a useful one in discussing *Les Thibault.*[4] The purely dramatic or scene presentation is, of course, illustrated by *Jean Barois.* A pictorial view is essentially an overview of a story in which a narrator summarizes and explains what happens, without our directly seeing the scenes and the confrontations, so that his view dominates. Clearly, novelists use a combination of these tactics. Like James and Flaubert, Martin du Gard relies on the scene to carry much of the weight of the novel. The opening episode of *Les Thibault* is a direct view of a family crisis, with a minimum of explanation by the author. Though Martin du Gard reverts from time to time to exposition, summarizing, and panoramic views of his characters' lives, past and present, he never relies wholly for long on this narrative voice which, while able to present a large collection of facts and sweep over time and place, does not have the dramatic impact, the *presence,* of a scene acted out. He recognized that his most natural device was the scene and that he excelled in giving the illusion of life, in making characters talk and act. "The only thing which I know how to do more or less well is to put the reader in direct contact with the scene that I am describing for him; in order to give life to my characters, it is usually sufficient for me to let them act and talk. As soon as I am obliged to comment on a character or analyze a feeling, I experience difficulty . . ."

(I, cxvii). "This truth of the narration is, I think, a natural gift; I feel capable of giving this degree of truth to everything I write. Besides, is it a gift? It is by application, by concentration of mind and imagination . . . that I succeed in making things seem true" (I, cxxvii). This is an accurate view of his own fictional qualities.

Like his master Tolstoy, Martin du Gard thus manages to handle an abundance of material and simultaneous threads of action with an apt use of dramatic and pictorial view, alternating. He isolates from the trajectory of his principal characters (much as Racine did) those episodes, those days which are crucial, prepares them and lets them give us directly the impressions which otherwise would be lengthy developments, or unimpressive details, in expository style. The contrast between the summarized actions and the scenes acted out directs our attention, develops our understanding of what the novel is pointing to, and involves us. It also creates a particular fictional rhythm. Although the structure of the novel can be called free,[5] it is not loose or without its own rhythm.

Balzac and Zola had grouped together numerous volumes under encompassing titles: *La Comédie humaine, les Rougon-Macquart*. The *roman-fleuve*, which has a single organic structure, is however a twentieth-century creation in France. Romain Rolland organized his *Jean-Christophe* around an individual, as Proust used an individual and a sensibility in *A la Recherche du temps perdu;* Georges Duhamel's *Pasquier* series, which is posterior to Martin du Gard's work, centers on a family like *Les Thibault. Les Hommes de bonne volonté*, the long fresco by Jules Romains, has unity of view but no consistent heroes, and it is organized around a probing of society in the first decades of the century. André Maurois has observed that Martin du Gard, instead of just revealing society in his novel, asks, "What is the meaning of this? Does it have a meaning? What is the value of suffering?"[6] Like all great fiction, his work is a philosophical reflection on human life; but the ideological element is subordinated to the concrete situations in which men reflect, and act, on the world about them.

Martin du Gard builds *Les Thibault* around two families, one more central than the other. The narration moves chronologically, with occasional flashbacks but few other interruptions in the forward movement. There remains no trace of the impressionistic, cinematographic technique of *Jean Barois*. Yet in *L'Eté 1914*, he achieves a semblance of simultaneous action by the detail with which he follows political developments all over the European continent and the rapidity of the action. The structure of the family into generations serves as another device for organization: not only are fathers and sons a theme, they are foci of action and movement, frequently directed at each other.

The point of view which is used throughout *Les Thibault*, with the exception of part of the *Epilogue*, consisting of Antoine's diary, is that which is called "neutral omniscience" in Norman Friedman's now-classic study of the concept of point of view.[7] It consists of potential, and sometimes demonstrated, omniscience concerning the actions and thoughts, past and present, of the characters—without, however, those intrusions of the author which characterize what Friedman calls "editorial omniscience." Like Flaubert and Maupassant, and like the majority of contemporary novelists, Martin du Gard avoids authorial interventions and adheres to the principle of impersonality—the so-called impassibility—of the French realists. He did not care for the nonchalance with which Gide, after Fielding and Stendhal, intruded as author to make comments on the book he was writing. With the neutral omniscient viewpoint, the novelist has the range of knowledge which he needs and the prerogative of moving in time and space and placing his authorial viewpoint in the consciousness of any personage or several. As Friedman shows, however, this prerogative can be finely manipulated to give, according to the needs, a greater or lesser impression of narrative authority. In some of the dramatic scenes, whose role has been discussed, Martin du Gard acts (as in *Jean Barois*) like a camera, recording only what can be seen and heard by an observer. In other passages, he concentrates on the mind of one character, limiting his omniscience and channeling all through this person's vision.

There is no doubt that this latter technique is responsible for some of the most acute and striking portraits of the volume. Scenes where Jacques or Antoine, in particular, are at the center of the action and are also the reflecting consciousness (reflecting usually on themselves, though not always so) give us the double sensitivity of the character's observations and of his own feelings. As Martin du Gard had remarked concerning the dramatic technique of his earlier novel, it would not have been feasible to handle the panoramic action and the wide cast of characters of *Les Thibault* using throughout a limited point of view, such as that of a witness or a protagonist; the story would have turned into a much narrower study. The neutral omniscient viewpoint is therefore the most practical; and, within it, deliberate reduction on occasions of the scope of the unseen narrator's knowledge leads to concentration of psychological portraiture and of sensibility.

The mirror which Martin du Gard, like Stendhal's novelist, moves along a road is turned both inward and outward. Knowledge of the human heart is his chief goal throughout the book. The novelist begins with this knowledge, of course; and Martin du Gard, unlike certain of his contemporaries, had in mind the precise line of development for each character. Yet the gradual creation of the characters must have led him to new insights into their possibilities, and to a richer view of their developing relationships. In 1931, a critic wrote in the *Mercure de France*, after stating that Martin du Gard was probably the most outstanding fictional writer of the time, that he "lets the elements of his narrative develop according to the character of the persons who are involved . . . His protagonists reveal themselves to him during the events, or rather, he takes full consciousness of their complexity as the circumstances oblige them to exteriorize their qualities and their faults."[8] Gide thought that "one of his Thibaults is living in him, with the result that it is less Roger who is speaking, than Antoine . . . it does not seem to me that the author is controlling his character here, nor that he can escape from him much."[9] This intensity of fictional life for the author (which recalls Balzac's) has, in any case, happy results, for the thoroughness with which we are led to understand Antoine and Jacques and Daniel, and the impression of psychological truth, are exemplary.

Some critics have felt that there is not enough imagination in these psychological studies, and Gide accused his friend of absence of interest in the unusual, of remaining too close to the typical.[10] It might be answered that his characters have that classical quality of being both exceptional and typical. Surely M. Thibault is not an ordinary character; but his qualities of authoritarianism, sanctimoniousness, bigotry, and fear are common ones, carried to a high degree. Jacques and Daniel are adolescents like many others formed at the same time, with a literary education, in the bourgeois world; however, Jacques, without being freakish like Lafcadio in *Les Caves du Vatican*, is highly individualistic, capable of extreme commitment and violent action.

Interest in individual psychology (criticized, of course, by Marxist commentators and praised by those who think a novel is essentially a portrait of individuals) does not keep Martin du Gard from turning his mirror to the world of the collectivity, particularly when his individuals can be taken as representatives of a group (as, for instance, we can read the case of the Protestant Mme de Fontanin) and as the younger heroes become involved in the social and political questions of the second decade of the century. He remains, however, more nearly a moralist in the seventeenth century sense than a student of sociology; *mœurs* are subordinated to *caractère*. Yet, as with Proust, we feel that the specimen can lead us to the species.

Through Antoine, we enter the world of upper-class medical circles and men of science; through M. Thibault, we glimpse the *bourgeoisie bien-pensante* with all its vanity, self-righteousness, and power; there are several clerics, a number of Protestants, students, men of politics, and in particular, representatives of the left-wing. Even with respect to women, Martin du Gard opens nearly the entire spectrum, from the pure and prudish Fontanins, to the women who live for pleasure like Rachel, to the sexless Mlle de Waize. No representatives of the lower classes appear in their own milieu, but among the secondary characters, there are a number, like M. Thibault's secretary M. Chasle, M. Faîsme, the director of the delinquent home, and Arthur, a servant there, and two waifs whom Antoine befriends, who bring, in the still caste-divided world of France around 1910, the speech and the attitudes of the unprivileged. What Martin du Gard has presented is a *choice* of characters from

the ranks of Parisian society and the milieux where the younger
Thibaults branch out—none of whom can be read as a stereotype
but who, together, create one of the keenest and most alive
views of France in the decades before the war. As in *Jean
Barois,* the author's documentation is thorough, and his allusions to public opinion, to the atmosphere of France, to modes
of living can be taken as reliable.

One of the areas of the novelist's attention is self-knowledge.
The long tradition of introspective fiction and drama in France
is pursued in much of *Les Thibault.* Jacques especially, Antoine,
and even M. Thibault are obsessed with their own images, de-
sirous to know and judge themselves. It is no wonder, from
this viewpoint, that Gide and Martin du Gard, while using
different techniques, could admire heartily each other's fiction.
The question, *Qui suis-je?* will continue to plague Antoine so
much that his journal will be a meditation on it. Generally,
the characters look to an examination of conscience, in the
Christian tradition, to give them the answer. Jacques will
choose finally a more nearly existentialist course, creating the
answer to who he is by what he does. The women of the novel
are in a subordinate position on this count: their questioning
of themselves is much less developed, since to a considerable
extent they take for granted the values and the definitions
which men have bestowed upon them.

Another facet of the human heart and human behavior which
plays a major role in *Les Thibault* is the relationships between
people. Martin du Gard's choice to make his heroes members
of tight family groups, and to have Jacques love women who
have grown up around him intensifies the possibilities for his
study of fruitful, pathetic, and tragic human relationships. The
range of his study is much wider than the family, however, particularly as the Thibaults grow older. "Among modern French
novels, only *A la Recherche du temps perdu* contains as intricate a range of relationships . . ."[11] As in *Jean Barois* and
Devenir!, few ties between human beings seem creative and
honest. Hypocrisy is not, perhaps, so rampant as in Gide's pension Vedel-Azaïs; but real communication is rare, and there is
constant irony created by the interplay between the ostensible
feelings of the characters for one another and their real isola-

tion. The solitude in which Jacques and Antoine both die and in which Daniel will be forced to live is the final face of their life-long moral solitude.

III   Le Cahier Gris

Le Cahier gris is one of the keenest portraits of adolescence in all of French literature. At the same time it is an introduction to the drama of two families, the Thibaults and the Fontanins, originally without connection but whose destinies will remain associated throughout a generation. In one volume Martin du Gard achieves the gradual exposition of the circumstances of the two families, the development of their relationships, the oblique portrait of several adults, and a close study of the two adolescents, Jacques Thibault and Daniel Fontanin, and their drama. The time of the action is not stated explicitly; but one can surmise that it is about 1905.[12] Since the volume opens with Monsieur Thibault and his elder son Antoine (nine years older than Jacques) and closes with a letter from Jacques to Daniel, the chief focus is on the Thibault family and Jacques in particular. The heart of the volume is the story of Jacques' and Daniel's flight from home, their adventures in Marseille, and the end of their escapade, which will bear life-long consequences for Jacques.

The story begins in the midst of a family drama, and all the opening exposition is done indirectly, progressively. The immediate emotional involvement of the reader is with Jacques; yet he does not appear directly for some pages. His father and brother are caught by the novelist through abrupt, excited dialogue: they have gone to Jacques' private school (where he has lessons after classes at the lycée) to see why he has not returned from what he had told them was an obligatory Sunday work session; and they learn that Jacques had lied, that he had not appeared at the school at all. The director is then forced to tell M. Thibault what has recently happened concerning Jacques, and what may throw light on his disapperance. He had been caught with a number of forbidden books—Rousseau's *Confessions*, a novel by Zola—and the director had also confiscated a notebook containing a clandestine correspondence between him and a certain "D." who, it is discovered, is a fellow pupil at the lycée. Discovering the confiscation, Jacques had caused a dreadful scene. The priest suggests clearly that the correspondence revealed a friendship anything but pure. By his violent reaction to this account, his moralistic comments and his anger, M. Thibault reveals one of the principal sides of his nature, which will play a conclusive role in subsequent episodes. Martin du Gard makes little use here of the privilege of the omniscient author to enter into his characters' consciousness; most of the scene is done through dialogue and simple observation.

Similarly, in our first glimpse of the Fontanin household, Daniel is the center of attention, without being present. The novelist makes an artful switch to the scene where Mme de Fontanin, anxious about her son, discovers that he has lied in the note he left her, questions her daughter Jenny about him, and spends the night waiting until, early the next morning, Antoine Thibault comes to tell her that Daniel and Jacques have apparently gone off together. By their reactions to this discovery, we see the nervous, fragile nature of Jenny, and the mother's strength and nobility as well as her Protestant faith and her belief in certain mystic phenomena. Her sentiment of superiority is not entirely reassuring to the reader, whose interest is attracted by the absent Daniel, the *révolté*. However, when she confronts M. Thibault in the following scene—in the hope of joining her efforts to his in a search—and when he scorns her from the height of his own feeling of superiority, the reader's sympathies are entirely for her. M. Thibault reveals himself as a sanctimonious Catholic who believes the worst about Protestants generally and who has accepted without any examination the priests' contentions that Daniel de Fontanin was responsible for leading Jacques astray. Throughout succeeding volumes he will appear as a Pharisee, bigoted and authoritarian; only by subtle touches will Martin du Gard gradually reveal to us (as though we were learning to *know* a person after having supposed he was as he first appeared) the man behind the self-righteous father: a fundamentally affectionate man, unhappy, afraid of death, and needing his sons' love.

Mme de Fontanin, who has been again abandoned by her husband, chronically unfaithful and remiss in his financial obligations, goes to inquire of his whereabouts from her cousin Noémie Petit-Dutreuil who, she discovers, has had a liaison with him which she never suspected. In this *scène à faire*, both the maternal devotion of Mme de Fontanin, and her womanly heart which has been wounded by her husband, appear in contrast to the other woman's indifference; but the latter is feigned, and we learn that Jérôme de Fontanin has deceived her also and left her bitter. It is to Martin du Gard's credit that these scenes are not melodramatic. His sober and careful style, and his convincing portrait of Mme de Fontanin as a woman of integrity, keep the confrontation from becoming vulgar.

Two days later, when nothing yet has been heard from the adolescents, Jenny is seriously ill with fever, and Mme de Fontanin receives the visit of her *pasteur*,[13] the Christian Scientist James Gregory. That Jenny's illness is in part psychosomatic will be revealed later when we discover that she has known all along Daniel's secret and has suffered at keeping it from her mother. Perhaps it is not surprising, then, that Gregory succeeds apparently in calming and curing her by faith-healing.

His technique is, however, contrasted with the steps that Antoine is taking to cure the girl. Antoine, who has a thoroughly positivistic view of men and the world, had already introduced himself to Mme de Fontanin as a doctor; here, we see him in his role—one of the crucial ones of the novel, through which Martin du Gard presents his view of medicine, his understanding of a scientific education and of the scientific view of the world, and his conception of professional integrity and devotion. Gregory's excitement and near-fanaticism (the novelist uses the adjective *maniaque*), his utter certainty that his belief is correct (a certainty which Antoine criticizes, much as Martin du Gard condemns generally those who believe to hold exclusively all truth—though Antoine of course is just as committed to his own view) contrast with the deliberate, rational approach of the doctor(I, 611-13). The outcome, of course, is ambiguous, since it can be due to Antoine's prescriptions as much as to Gregory's prayers. Martin du Gard leaves it ambivalent; but the general context of the novel throws a critical light on the belief of Gregory and Mme de Fontanin.

It is only after these revealing scenes that we begin to know Daniel and Jacques, through extracts from the gray notebook which had caused so much consternation among the priests. In language which reveals their idealism, their thirst for communion, and their literary background, the two adolescents have written to each other lyrical declarations of eternal friendship and commitment to high ideals. As Justin O'Brien has shown in his study of the novel of adolescence, this is a superior portrait of the friendship of two boys, intelligent, sensitive, whose literary education is highly developed but who are locked in a narrow world, without experience, and (in the case of Jacques), deprived of maternal love and paternal understanding.[14] Nothing in the context suggests that this friendship is opprobrious in any way; it is, however, clearly characteristic of the time of puberty before sexual interests are definitely fixed on the opposite sex. When Jacques and Daniel have experiences with girls, their own friendship will become less important to them. One can read here a criticism of the bourgeois world in which they are growing up and being educated, whose confines are unrealistically narrow.[15]

After the letters from the notebook which show their intimacy in a different light from the interpretation that M. Thibault gives, the two boys appear in a flashback showing them at Marseille after their trip from Paris. They are presented by third-person description and by their conversations. The difficulty of their position and the uncertainty of adolescence are brought out well as the author contrasts their determination and their self-knowledge, on the one hand, with their dependence on each other, on their luck (which shortly runs out), and, ultimately, on society.

Martin du Gard uses some physical description, by fine touches, but concentrates more on the characters of the two boys—their resemblances and their differences. Daniel, who looks older and seems more self-assured, is in reality less determined than his friend, who is a year younger, and less often makes the decisions. Without confessing it to Jacques, he is torn by worry over his mother and sister and remorse for leaving them, and his attempts to embark with Jacques to Africa become half-hearted. Two of Daniel's fundamental features—his affection for his mother and his sentimentality—thus come into play early. Jacques, on the other hand, reveals no scruples about running from his father. His problems are only of a practical nature: how to get onto a boat and out to sea without being caught. His resentment against his masters and his father leaves no room for regret. One thinks of Stendhal's observation, "Nos parents et nos maîtres sont nos ennemis naturels." After failing to smuggle themselves onto a boat, the two boys become separated. Jacques falls to sleep among bales piled on the wharves—a scene which will have its counterpart in *L'Eté 1914* when Jacques lies dying. Daniel is taken in by a young woman, who gives him his first experience of physical love, thus creating a secret which he cannot share with Jacques. The following day the boys witness a scene of human and animal misery which fascinates Jacques and reveals in him the capacity to be moved by others unknown to him, foreshadowing his later commitment to socialism. The next day, the boys are picked up at an inn by the local police and sent back to Paris.

The source of Daniel's sentimentality is revealed in the following scene, in Paris, where Jérôme de Fontanin returns temporarily to the Fontanin household, inquires about his son and his sick daughter, swears his repentance and begs for mercy from his wife. Martin du Gard's conviction that heredity plays a preponderant role in character has made him give to Daniel some of the weakness and the emotionalism of the father. At the same time, Mme de Fontanin's character is illuminated, both by her reaction (severe and controlled) to her pleading husband, whom she sends away for the night, and to Daniel when he reappears. He is welcomed into the house with affection and kindness, without reproaches. Jacques and Antoine are witnesses to this scene. Mme de Fontanin's character is one of the most subtle of the whole novel, and our judgment on her cannot be without ambiguity. Here, at least, it is clear, from the admiration that everyone feels, that she represents an ideal of parental affection and charity which M. Thibault, by contrast, shows not at all to Jacques.

The scene of Jacques' return is a superior but humanly painful one, in which Martin du Gard maintains a quasi-objective authorial voice but throws a damning light on the family relationships of the Thibaults and on the father in particular. In this light, Jacques' rebellion seems justified. Throughout the novel he will remain something of a romantic hero, and the sympathy of both the reader and the author will remain at his side, even when his bad humor (which he recognizes) comes out, even when he is frantically individualistic and opposed to the more rational and socialized Antoine. Indeed, the "social cell" of the family, which the society depicted by Martin du Gard takes without question and which is the fundamental social structure, as well as a compositional feature, of the novel, is nonetheless called into question in the novel by the failure of the Thibaults and the Fontanins to maintain a family relationship that benefits all, and by the persistent criticism the family receives from sympathetic characters like Jacques. Martin du Gard must have been aware of the ambivalence of his portrait, which is constantly oriented to the bourgeois family but also oriented away from it, sometimes explosively. It is significant that, at the end, none of the younger generation will have founded acceptable families: Antoine and Daniel will have no children, Jacques' and Jenny's son is illegitimate.

In contrast to the open naturalness of the Fontanins, at the Thibault household, when Jacques returns, no one can speak truthfully and nothing is natural. Only the governess and housekeeper, Mademoiselle de Waize (who has been there since Mme Thibault died) and her young niece, Gise, can spontaneously show their pleasure at having Jacques back; and their role is too subordinate for this to count for much. It is true that Antoine is gentle with his younger brother and tries to assure him of his friendship, even praising his verse. But Jacques is afraid that his father, as well as Antoine, has read the notebook with the poems; this kills in him all feeling of duty and affection for his father, and he stands before him mute. M. Thibault longs for a word of repentance from the prodigal son, longs to admit that he loves the boy. In the face of his silence, he speaks like a magistrate, addressing himself only to Antoine and speaking of the measures he will take to assure that such an act of disobedience and ingratitude shall not recur. Even Abbé Vécard, who later will take up Jacques' defense, comes to scold him and does not realize that a boy in need of affection coexists with the rebel. At the end of *Le Cahier gris*, Jacques, who has gone to hear from his father what his punishment will be and learned that he will be sent away to a detention school, writes a passionate, pathetic letter to Daniel, to tell him that he will see him no longer and that, if the punishment is too severe, he will kill himself.

The ending of this part thus forms an immediate link to the next part, *Le Pénitencier* (the penitentiary or, in this case, home for delinquents); it also throws a sinister light on the principles of M. Thibault, or at least his success in carrying them out. He refers frequently to all he has done for his son and to his devotion to the family and to social order. No communication exists between him and Jacques, however, and little between him and his elder son. The discipline he plans for Jacques is not to be a family act, but rather to consist in placing authority for directing him in the hands of professional guardians. He appears, moreover, as a man much more occupied with his own self-righteousness than with the realities of human needs and relationships. Throughout the volume, the conflict of generations is developed and will continue to be central, assuming political form in *L'Eté 1914*.

Le Cahier gris, like most of the succeeding parts, cannot be called a novel in itself, since the materials which it proposes are not dealt with completely and its problems are left unsolved. Nevertheless, it does have fictional unity, as well as being a beginning for long subsequent developments. The action lasts a few days: from Sunday, date of the boys' departure, to the end of the week when Jacques is told his sentence. It revolves quite equally around three groups—the Thibaults, the Fontanins, and Jacques and Daniel—among whom there are ties of relationship and of action. Character is shown, not just described, and is carried beyond the first acquaintance; yet no character is presented exhaustively, and that element of mystery, of shadow, which Gide wanted Martin du Gard to develop in his work, surrounds M. Thibault, Daniel, M. de Fontanin, even Jenny, and particularly Jacques, in whom we suspect recesses of action and feeling which will draw him far from the limits circumscribed in this volume.

IV   Le Pénitencier

As the focus and the ending of the preceding volume would suggest, Jacques is at the center of *Le Pénitencier*. He is the character whose life is at once most dramatic and most full of promises. His position in the structure of the two families is likewise pivotal. In the course of this part, nearly all the characters who have previously appeared return, not gratuitously but because Jacques' drama involves them. Thematically, this part pursues themes adumbrated in part I: the family and adolescence. To them are added the themes of belief, sincerity, and young love, which likewise have been foreshadowed. Although the action extends over several months and is more episodic than in *Le Cahier gris*, there remains a unity of tone, of concern, and of character which prevents the volume from having the fragmented quality of an interminable serial novel.

The first half of this part concerns Jacques' situation in the detention home and Antoine's efforts to get him out. It is with amazement that the reader learns that the penitentiary at Crony is a philanthropic work of M. Thibault himself. He had conceived of this institution and created it with the help of the archdiocese of Paris. However, Jacques does not enter under ordinary arrangements. He is put under special discipline, by which he is alone all the time except for an occasional lesson and the company of his guard, and he is virtually confined to his cell.

As the book opens, it is March of the following year, and Jacques has been there for nearly nine months. M. Thibault has paid only routine visits to the colony and has scarcely seen his son. Antoine has not had the privilege of visiting at all. Indeed, the reader knows practically nothing about Jacques' situation, except for these few facts. Antoine, however, has been reflecting on the situation. A chance meeting with Daniel the previous day has led him to return to the Fontanin household to find out whether Daniel has heard from Jacques. Indeed, he has, but the notes are brief and, moreover, misleading, since he speaks of being at a boarding school and of enjoying the company of his schoolmates. Antoine wonders what has prompted him to lie thus, and his suspicions are kindled. The reader begins to share these suspicions; indeed, the arrangement begins to sound cruel and to evoke memories of Dickens' novels, Balzac's *Louis Lambert,* and other tales of mistreatment of schoolboys. Antoine decides to visit the colony without his father's knowledge, and to discover the truth. Though he had accepted his father's arguments about the value of isolation as a punishment, he now regrets this agreement.

Through Antoine's reflections, Martin du Gard skillfully manipulates the reader's curiosity and fears, and we anticipate dreadful discoveries. Since, however, this is the twentieth century, and since M. Thibault and his fellow philanthropists are not sadistic, though considerably short-sighted, what Antoine manages to find out is not sensational and is reprehensible only in two instances. There is little physical punishment used at the school, and Jacques has been the object of no special privations except that of companionship and responsible professors. Martin du Gard refuses to develop the possible sordidness of such a situation, except in one respect (which by itself is serious enough). The first of his two guardians had shown no sense of responsibility and had amused the boy by showing him, and then having him copy and imagine, obscene drawings. When this man was replaced by a fellow called Arthur, Jacques was no better off: the latter, Jacques insinuates to his brother, has pederastic inclinations. In an embarrassing scene after Antoine has left, Arthur makes what are clearly suggestive remarks. Martin du Gard keeps these episodes under tight stylistic control—which is necessary to keep them from becoming a melodramatic, sensational revelation and which, moreover, is faithful to the conception of the characters, for Jacques is terribly embarrassed about his situation and about the revelations which he makes to Antoine, in his fatigue and his loneliness. Nevertheless, we are reminded of Diderot's *La Religieuse,* and M. Thibault's sanctimonious pride in the school receives a damning qualification.

It is only with difficulty, through two different interviews, that Antoine manages to draw the truth from his brother. At first the latter is so reticent that Antoine thinks he will have to leave without seeing at all what his life is really like. This is not because Jacques has been morally corrupted by the atmosphere of his corridor and the whole school. Again, Martin du Gard refuses the facile psychology of clear-cut evil or sordidness. Jacques has not even been clearly brainwashed. He has, however, suffered from lack of exercise, meager diet, rapid adolescent growth in these circumstances, and absence of companionship, of dialogue with any decent human being or person his own age. His energies and his will have been worn down: he chooses the simplest solution, that of acceptance, not protesting, not even wishing to leave the school which, after all, offers its own kind of security. The strength of his earlier revolt against his father, and the intensity of the memory, can be understood best, perhaps, when Jacques states bluntly that he much prefers remaining in the detention home to returning to live in his real home.

This recognition, more than any particular fact about the school administration (except for the question of the guardians) moves Antoine to confront his father and plead with him to release Jacques. This is the first instance of a confrontation of the elder son with his father—the two Thibault personalities, with their obstination and their force, matching each other. M. Thibault refuses, of course, any suggestion that he might have been mistaken in choosing that discipline for his son, and that the operation of the school might not be just as regular as he imagines it. Antoine has to have recourse to Abbé Vécard, who wins some of the reader's sympathy in listening, understanding, and agreeing to help.

M. Thibault, who is accustomed to manipulating others, is here manipulated in his turn by his confessor, through his pride and his vanity. The abbé is not as rigid in his views on rearing children as M. Thibault is; nor is he a man of such principles that he will not make a politic use of someone's weaknesses for what he believes is a good cause. Antoine had conceived the scheme of bringing Jacques back, not to live in the Thibault household but to take up residence with him in the new quarters which he is shortly going to occupy in the same building, where he can receive his patients. Agreeing with the wisdom of this, the priest subtly suggests it to M. Thibault as a means of having Jacques back without losing face and without being responsible for discipline, which Antoine would take over. If the priest had proposed this at first, M. Thibault would not have agreed, for he was in the beginning closed to all suggestions. But the priest subtly works on his pride (M. Thibault is shortly to be elected to the Institut de France), his fear of God's judgment (he reads the parable of the prodigal son)—in short, his humility and vanity, doubt and belief. The entire episode can be read as a study in hypocrisy and self-deception (Gide's dictum, "Le vrai hypocrite est celui qui se ment à lui-même," can be applied to M. Thibault) and in the failure of self-deception when, as in Sartrian psychology, a judgment is brought to bear from the exterior. This foreshadows the episodes before M. Thibault's death in which, his confidence abandoning him (as with Barois), his real self is revealed, cringing (see I, 733).

Jacques returns, then, to inaugurate with Antoine his new quarters. Martin du Gard gives us short sketches of all the household as this change is being made—Mlle de Waize and Gise as well as the principal characters. And we see Antoine in a new light, independent from his father, living in his own *garçonnière*, and embarking on a career which, he has no doubt, will be splendid. There is a fine passage in which he reflects on what it means to be a Thibault:

We are two brothers. That doesn't seem important, and yet it is a very new thing for me, very serious. Brothers! Not only the same blood, but the same roots from the beginning of the ages . . . And what is terrible, is to have in oneself this spirit . . . the spirit of the Thibaults. . . . Wherever I've been, at school, at the university, at the hospital, everywhere I have felt that I was a Thibault, someone apart, I won't say superior, but yes, why not? superior, armed with a force which others don't have. (I, 763)

The life that Antoine and Jacques lead has something of the freshness and the sense of freedom of youth; Antoine's energy and belief in himself make up for Jacques' moments of moodiness, of anger at himself and others, and for his lack of goal; Jacques' idealism forms a counterpart to Antoine's practical sense and more mature outlook.

During these months, Jacques has his first love affair. The raptures which he feels for his concierge's niece, Lisbeth Fruhling, recall those of the young Jean Barois before Cécile. Martin du Gard shows the gradual birth of feeling in him, his shyness in front of Lisbeth, his determination to call her his fiancée, his awkward, limited gestures of affection. It is to be observed that Jacques does not dream of consummating his love with her physically: there is in him the predisposition, frequent among adolescents and extremely important in the biographies of Baudelaire, Gide, and others, towards dissociation of physical and intellectual or ideal love (I, 773). This idyll has, unfortunately, a less attractive facet: through a short scene between Lisbeth and Antoine, we learn that the latter, who in a rather clinical way has been the recipient of her favors, has also encouraged her to seduce Jacques, hoping presumably to assist in his initiation to love. In any case, the attempt fails, and Lisbeth returns to her uncle's in Alsace.

The remaining chapters of *Le Pénitencier* are focused on Jacques and on the Fontanins. Although M. Thibault has forbidden Jacques to have any dealing with the Fontanins (whom he considers responsible for corrupting his son), Jacques has written to Daniel, and Antoine learns of it. After a scene, Antoine consents to let his younger brother visit Daniel, and they both go the following Sunday. Before they arrive, we witness a conversation between Pastor Gregory and Mme de Fontanin. Gregory comes on behalf of the husband, who asks pardon and begs that his wife not pursue her divorce suit. The impression of fanaticism that he gave in *Le Cahier gris* is reinforced here: if Martin du Gard criticizes M. Thibault's bigotry, surely the Protestantism of Gregory is just as unattractive. Though the man obviously has charitable intentions, his insistence that Mme de Fontanin take back a husband who has not supported her or her children with any regularity and who has repeatedly betrayed her to her face, seems unwise and unkind to her. His own story, which he tells as an example, is an extreme instance of turning the other cheek.

When the Thibaults arrive, there is a kind of pairing-off ballet between them and Mme de Fontanin, Daniel, Jenny, and Mme de Fontanin's cousin's daughter, Nicole, who has left her

mother's irregular household to come live with the Fontanins.
The meeting between Jacques and Daniel is unsatisfactory; too
many things have been left untold, and now there is between
them Jacques' interest in Lisbeth and Daniel's aggressive interest
in his cousin Nicole. (It is still another comment on heredity
that Daniel should pursue the daughter of his father's mistress.)
Antoine and Mme de Fontanin (whom he admires) converse
while Daniel and Nicole are alone in a darkroom, quarreling
because she repulses his advances; in another room are Jacques
and Jenny, neither of whom is attracted to the other physically
but who are vaguely interested in asserting themselves over the
other. As the adolescents make unkind remarks to each other,
Antoine tells Mme de Fontanin about his own religious position
—lack of belief and a scientific view of the world (I, 796). This
is obviously an image of Martin du Gard's own scientific agnos-
ticism (see I, 569-70), and it reinforces our feeling that, without
being an autobiographic hero, Antoine is frequently close to the
author's own personality and belief. At the end of this discussion, moved by a sense of her own wrongs, Mme de Fontanin
writes a note to Gregory announcing that she will pardon
Jérôme.

In the final episode of this part, Lisbeth returns for the concierge's funeral and Jacques, not knowing that her stay will be
brief, experiences a renascence of his love for her. This time,
however, he completes the caresses of love; it is a new stage in
his adolescent development, and it is an appropriate time for
Le Pénitencier to close.

Throughout this volume, like the preceding, Martin du Gard
uses, with discretion, the omniscient point of view which will be
his principal technique throughout the novel. In certain episodes, however, he uses a limited-view third person viewpoint—
the viewpoint of an observer only, with no entry into the
consciousness of the characters. In others, he uses limited
omniscience—that is, the relating of thoughts from the mind of
one person only. Occasionally we are struck by a change in
viewpoint, as during Antoine's visit to the penitentiary: most
of the episode is recounted from Antoine's point of view only,
with his thoughts and speculations, but there are sudden
switches when the author enters into Jacques' thoughts (I, 706),

This has the obvious advantage of correcting Antoine's reflections by those of Jacques, who is at the center of interest; but it breaks the illusion that we are there, as Antoine, trying to piece together Jacques' situation and attitude from what we can observe. This is, I believe, one of the few pages where the author has made a technical choice which detracts more than it adds. In other scenes, the handling of the omniscient viewpoint is highly skillful, with a sense of *vraisemblance*, of objective narration, and yet of a center of interest on one or more characters whose consciousness is brought to the forefront.

Claude Roy calls the first pages of *Le Pénitencier* "an admirable portrait of the awkward age."[16] Robert Gibson wrote, "Militant idealism, the determination never to compromise alternating with profound world-weariness, self-dramatization and self-pity, the whole process of erotic awakening, from the tormented reveries of lonely puberty, through ethereal first love, to sexual initiation—nearly every twentieth century novelist of note, from Colette to Camus, has examined one or other of these adolescent traits in isolation: none has integrated them all so successfully into a single complex study . . ."[17] The first two volumes are an excellent study of adolescent aspirations and possibilities—what Martin du Gard called earlier "becoming." It develops the opposition between Antoine, who is channeling his forces, both his virtues and his egoism, in a socially acceptable way and who therefore can look forward to self-expression without dispersion of his energies in revolt; and Jacques, whose need for self-expression has been ignored and whose energies are dominating him, rather than he them—who shows promise but no taste yet for directing his desires, no understanding of the viewpoint of others. M. Thibault's egoism as well as his personal force, plus the unknown heredity from the mother, have combined in the two brothers but taken in each case a different form. At the end of this part, the reader can suppose that the help Antoine is giving his brother, and the freedom the latter has to see his friends, to read and study away from his father, may lead to a new adaptibility in him. At the beginning of the following volume, Martin du Gard will reveal how many of these hopes have been fulfilled, as Jacques reaches the age of twenty.

CHAPTER 5

Les Thibault: La Belle Saison
and La Consultation

I La Belle saison

THE longest of the volumes before *L'Eté 1914*, *La Belle saison* contains both concentration of the fictional material, around previously-introduced material, and expansion of the novelist's view, in society and in range of thematic material. As before, the action radiates principally around the two *foyers*, the Thibaults (Antoine and Jacques, this time, rather than the father) and the Fontanins, into whom we receive much new insight, thanks mainly to several chapters concerning Jérôme de Fontanin. Because both of the families have summer homes at Maisons-Lafitte, not far from Paris, it serves as a geographic point of organization, to which the narrative returns after episodes have taken place elsewhere. The narrative is in general a straight time sequence; but since Martin du Gard is handling several stories at once, there are jumps and interruptions. There is, thus, a sense of simultaneous action: Jacques and Jenny are engaged in certain activities, while, we later learn, Antoine is pursuing his affair and M. de Fontanin is involved in a drama with his wife and mistress. The example of Tolstoy must have been useful in helping Martin du Gard organize the material in this part.

It is appropriate that, as Jacques and Daniel are growing into young men, and Antoine is a young professional man, unmarried, the novelist should turn his attention from the upper bourgeois milieu in which they were raised to classes beyond that society. This is not, of course, another *Côté de Guermantes* in which the narrator penetrates into social circles far above his original ones (though there is here a study of manners like that of

Proust): rather, Daniel and especially Antoine penetrate into a *demi-monde* where the values are the reverse of what they have held previously and where they discover a kind of drama foreign to their upbringing. There are even insights into the world of the petty bourgeoisie, through M. Chasle, the secretary of M. Thibault, who lives with his tyrannic mother and an old servant.

The title, both descriptive and ironic, points to one of the themes of the volume: youth, its freedom and its beauty. Like the two preceding parts, *La Belle saison* is a *Bildüngsroman.* Daniel, Jenny, Jacques, Antoine, and even some of the secondary characters are variations on the theme. There is a tremendous sense of possibility. Daniel has unmistakable talent in art and is engaged in art publication as well as his own work; Jacques has just passed the entrance examination into the Ecole Normale (France's professional school for the highest intellects); Antoine has his own practice as well as lectures to give as a specialist in pediatrics. The perspectives seem limitless.

Each principal character, however, gives to these possibilities his own qualification, which appears as the reverse side of human potentiality, as a sort of fatality pointing to the ultimate dead-end of death, never far from Martin du Gard's preoccupations. Antoine's sense of fatality is the least tragic. Although he feels himself destined for a successful career in medicine, he also experiences a need for adventure, for action outside the bounds of his profession; yet he knows that he will not grant himself this, will not depart from his direct line toward professional success, or from the bourgeois values dictated by his rearing.

Daniel's qualification is obviously that of heredity. Throughout Martin du Gard's novels rings the insistence on heredity—usually with the tragic overtones of the Greek drama. Suggestions that Daniel was like his father occurred in earlier volumes. In *La Belle saison,* he is clearly the image of Jérôme, morally and physically—an attractive philanderer, thinking of his own pleasure, ready to seduce any attractive object. This is brought out by a cruel, but not improbable coincidence, when Daniel seduces a young woman whom his father had previously kept as a mistress, who is enamored of the son because he resembles his father. In Martin du Gard, as in Molière and Proust, people are punished where they have erred: his fate in the war will be to lose his virility.

As for Jacques, the qualification is probably likewise due to heredity, but not in such an obvious way. His case of *Weltschmertz* cannot be clearly tied to any feature in his father's makeup; yet it is suggested at various moments throughout the novel that Antoine and Jacques both represent their father's potentiality, each in a different way. Certainly Jacques has suffered from his upbringing, from the absence of a maternal affection and the lack of understanding on his father's part. At this point, he is still at war, internally, with the society to which he gains a glorious admission by entrance into the Ecole Normale; he is not even happy about having passed the exams, and less about the prospect of becoming one of the intellect machines of the school. He dreams of leaving it all behind and escaping some place where he could be himself and write. Yet the cutting of the umbilical cord between himself and his bourgeois world is extremely difficult, much more so than for Daniel. Jacques has the moralism, the puritanism of his father, reinforced by his sensitive, poetic nature and his over-developed baggage of literary idealism. He cannot simply "épater le bourgeois" and have done with it; he does not join the Bohemian artists' world. When he revolts, it will be thorough-going and far-reaching and he will, literally, have to leave the country. Meanwhile, his promise, of which his family is proud, is at every step undermined by his own torments, his rebellion, his need to be singled out as different.

From the theme of "la belle saison" one is led to another principal theme of the volume, love. Bitter and sweet, sordid and idealistic, love appears in as many forms, and under as cruel a light, as in Proust's masterpiece, and each of these forms is a comment on the others. Daniel's experience is the lowest kind of liaison. It furnishes, nevertheless, the occasion for excellent portraits of the young Parisians who are kept by artists and business men and who lead a kind of *demi-monde* existence. Jérôme's affairs also furnish the portrait of another species of love, that between a married man and the mistress who has left her position and neglected her child in order to live with him.

This is Noémie, Mme de Fontanin's cousin. The reader does not see the trajectory of their five-year liaison. Instead, Martin du Gard presents the episode where Noémie is dying in Amsterdam. Mme de Fontanin, called there by her husband who is desperate for money and who, like other weakwilled people, cannot bear difficulty without some support, witnesses the last days and the burial of the woman who had taken her husband, and whose own life is ruined. The sense of human disaster, and of the failure of romantic love in this form, is very strong. The worst comment on the *liaison* comes from Jérôme, whose fundamental indifference to the dying woman, and relief when she is gone, are damning.

Mme de Fontanin's love for her husband is of still a different quality. In her are mixed a Christian sense of devotion to one's husband; a distaste for the man who, while playing on her sympathies, has abandoned her and neglected her children; and a strong attraction to the man Jérôme, as he appeared to her doubtless before their marriage and still appears at his better moments—charming and physically attractive. Martin du Gard renders well the ambiguity of her feelings: her determination and yet her susceptibility to the sensual appeal which she condemns. Even here, there is a sense of that fatality which is so strong with Daniel and Jacques.

The two most subtle studies of love concern Jacques and Jenny. Their ambivalent attraction for each other is a revelation of character. It is not because Jacques loves Jenny that he is the way he is; his character takes precedence, and it is because he is such that he is drawn toward Jenny. Throughout the scenes at Maisons-Lafitte, Jacques, undergoing a painful self-examination and experiencing dissatisfaction with his situation, is attracted by the enigmatic girl. He cannot express his interest with any graciousness; more often than not, he offends her. Only on a few occasions does he have full consciousness of this attraction. At those moments, he believes that he loves Jenny, ideally, with a love which is not of the world where Antoine and Daniel move. Jenny is less conscious of her own attraction toward Jacques. When she does come to the brink of consciousness, she refuses the knowledge and instead proclaims her hatred for everything pertaining to the Thibaults. She treats him badly and attributes to his gestures the worst motives. It is clear, of course, that this is the underside of her passionate love for him. It is equally clear that love—which she has observed in the relations between her father and mother, and through Daniel's loose life—is repellent to her. Very obviously she is fighting her own attraction; early in her life she is making herself into a woman who does not want love and who cannot give herself. It is possible that through this portrait Martin du Gard is attacking the Calvinistic ethic. He also shows one of the results of her environment upon her. (It can be pointed out that, among all the women in this chapter, there is none for whom love is not either a source of dread and an indication of weakness; a livelihood; or a perverted passion. As in Proust's work, a healthy, reciprocal love, both physical and moral, seems impossible.) It would seem to be part of Jacques' fatality that his cornelianism, as demanding as Jenny's very personal puritanism, cannot meet her at any point. The moments of understanding are rare, and Jenny withdraws from them rapidly. Without any authorial comment, the failure of human communication, even in pure love, is poignantly clear.

Antoine—ordinarily phlegmatic in his relationships with others, and willfully determined in his professional life—becomes personally involved with a woman for the first time. The story of his liaison occupies most of six chapters of the fourteen in *La Belle saison*. It holds considerable promise. Rachel is beautiful and appealing; she is clearly in love with him; she is free to do as she pleases and does not ask for marriage, nor interfere with his work. Though this is not the union of two perfectly attuned minds, Martin du Gard paints their relationship as affectionate and true. The accounts of some of their moments have a lyricism which hitherto was not associated with Antoine, the rational man.

Yet this love, too, is doomed to failure, not by the attrition of months and years, or by the romanticism of either partner (neither fails to be realistic), but by the perverted character of Rachel. The naturalists' taste for the sordid reappears here in Martin du Gard. It is not a matter, however, of local color or *mœurs du peuple*, but rather a study of the depths of the human heart. He has much more than a passing interest in the hidden dramas which reveal people in their psychological nakedness, beyond the limits of the socially permissible. Those who suggest (as Gide did) that his preoccupations were too exclusively with the ordinary, the norm, should recall this episode of Rachel, as well as *Vieille France* and *Confidence africaine*. Hirsch, Rachel's former lover, while not appearing in person anywhere in the volume, is represented by her in a powerful portrait as a sadistic, sexually perverted, hypnotic man. Rachel, for all her loveliness and her devotion to Antoine, is enchained to this man through her own desires, which are both masochistic and sadistic; when he calls her to him, she cannot help going. (Noteworthy for the understanding of heredity in *Les Thibault* is the fact that Rachel's mother is completely mad and that her brother had a suicide fixation.) Her knowledge that he slept with his own daughter and probably pushed her, as well as her husband, to suicide, does not mitigate her obedience to him. She is the "natural, therefore abominable" woman of Baudelaire.

As Martin du Gard develops his characters in this volume by what and whom they love, and by how they pursue their dreams, he also indicates something about them by what they are *not* concerned with. It is a severe, doubtless justified, indictment of their class and of their age that they should show no concern whatsoever with the political events of their time, or even with the wider circle of society and social problems around them. This is not, of course, just the gay world of *la belle époque;* on the contrary, a spirit of seriousness marks every principal character except Jérôme de Fontanin. But the seriousness is all turned inward. Even M. Thibault, with his philanthropy and charities, is much more aware of his own role, his own personage, than he is of the operation of his charities. He has his name legally changed to Oscar-Thibault (his first and last names) so that his sons may carry with them the *Oscar.* He is, moreover, obviously pleased when a cooperative manufacturing venture, supported by the Church, in which the workers were to divide the profits, fails. He applies his authoritarian approach to all problems, domestic and social. Jacques, Antoine, and Daniel are simply indifferent. The turnabout of Jacques to an ardent socialism will be all the more striking.

[93]

The episodes of this volume are too diverse and too numerous to be told in detail. The majority of them are concerned with the themes and the character development sketched above. Others present background figures who are associated with the lives of the chief characters, and can be considered scenes of manners as much as elements of the plot. Martin du Gard never extends too far, however, the privilege of the novelist to let his view linger on curious but unrelated scenes. When he brings in secondary figures and recounts their background, it is always with relationship to one of the principal characters and is a means of elucidating his reactions or the world in which he moves.

Certain crucial incidents deserve close attention, nevertheless. One of the most frequently cited episodes of *Les Thibault* is the opening scene of *La Belle saison* in which Jacques, on the way to the Ecole Normale with Antoine to see the exam results, tell his brother about the book where Daniel "has found all the excuses—worse, the glorification—for his cynicism . . . a book which burns your hands as you read it . . . " (I, 820). This is Gide's *Nourritures terrestres.* The discussion is followed by a retrospective expository passage in which we see Daniel discovering for the first time the book which becomes a sort of Bible for him. He is struck by the invitation to desire, by the refusal of tranquility, by the justification of a personal amoral code: "Il faut agir sans juger si l'action est bonne ou mauvaise." Jacques too responds to the force of the book, but he cannot accept what seems to him its cavalier attitude towards morality. This episode, reflecting Martin du Gard's admiration, was instrumental in attracting the attention of a whole generation of young readers to *Les Nourritures terrestres,* which had previously been virtually ignored.[1] The quotations and the reactions of the two young men set the tone for their actions and deliberations throughout the rest of the volume: Jacques' sensitivity to the appeal of the exotic and his resentment against his family, as well as his moralism (he quotes the famous "Familles, je vous hais"); Daniel's rejection of his family's code, and his pursuit of pleasure.[2]

The episode in which Antoine makes the acquaintance of Rachel is a skillfully handled treatment of a first meeting as well as a view of Antoine's competence as a doctor and his personal force. It is the first time that he is seen extensively in his professional role. He is like an artist, taking pride in his work, letting it speak for itself. Like Rachel, who watches fascinated, we are impressed with his skill; and his *amor fati*, his satisfaction (which recalls his father's self-satisfaction) at having chosen the medical profession and succeeded so young seems justified. Unlike a long line of predecessors, from Molière through Proust, Martin du Gard does not make the medical profession an object of mockery. Indeed, one feels that it must have been a *vocation manquée* for him. His close association with the positivistic views of the late nineteenth century can be induced from the value which he gives over and over to the work of doctors. One can also infer pessimism concerning the possibility of moral progress and the value of moral ideals, which seem so problematic compared to the concrete good done by the doctor. Antoine is involved during the novel in a number of incidents in which he saves life, whereas the ideals of Jenny, Mme de Fontanin, and M. Thibault apparently bear unfortunate fruit and, as Antoine reflects upon them, seem positively harmful. As *Jean Barois* seems to show, life is one of the few permanent values in Martin du Gard's work; even it will receive some qualification at the end of *Les Thibault*, but less so than any other ideal.

The episodes in which Jérôme de Fontanin appears, in the roles of ex-lover and husband, are well handled scenes in which potentially melodramatic material is controlled and where the portrait of Jérôme is admirably developed. He is a weak and sentimental man, who turns for his pleasure to other women but returns to his wife to find the support, approval, and forgiveness that he cannot find in himself. After Néomie's death, he feels that a great burden has been lifted from him. He comes back as though it were a matter of course to the family house at Maisons-Lafitte. Like Mme de Fontanin, however, one feels that it is only a matter of time before he will find a new pretext for leaving. This is rendered more likely as he convinces himself, bit by bit, that he is "better than his life." This is an excellent example of a variety of Sartrian *mauvaise foi*. Refusing to see that it is his acts—freely chosen (as far as our context goes)—that define him, he dissociates himself from what he has done and feels that the real Jérôme is somewhere else, noble, unappreciated, spiritually faithful to his wife. He picks up one day, at his Paris address, a two-year old letter from a young mistress whom he had left, unaware that she was pregnant. When he goes to visit her, he begs for her pardon. Then, when he has it: "Tears came to his eyes. It seemed to him that he was returning to the universal harmony . . . 'I'm good,' Jérôme repeated to himself. 'People judge me badly. They don't know. I'm better than my life'" (I, 1019). His gesture of sending Cricri back to Bretagne with a little income, as he seduces her once again, is a sentimentalist's attempt to buy respect.

After the scene of the operation, during which Antoine and Rachel meet for the first time, there is a series of episodes in which one sees both their developing love (Antoine seems transformed) and Rachel's past, in fragmented views but with its import increasingly clear. Though the material has a perverted and lascivious element, it is treated by Martin du Gard, through Rachel herself, either in a matter-of-fact manner or tragically—never melodramatically. She is caught up by her memories and reveals to Antoine crucial episodes in her liaison with Hirsch and in Hirsch's own past, as well as the story of her affair with a sadistic tenor and the child she bore him. Antoine and Rachel make a visit together to the tomb of the child in Normandy.

At this time, Rachel has already decided that she will return to Hirsch, although neither the reader nor Antoine knows it. Throughout the scene, one feels an indescribable malaise which is not just a result of the circumstances of the visit. Shortly thereafter, she tells Antoine that she will return to Africa—not stating, however, that Hirsch is waiting for her. Antoine endures the last month of their liaision in full view of his incapacity to change her mind. The episode of her departure is one of the finest of the volume. With little explanatory material, Martin du Gard shows scenically their last day together, in Le Havre, in the course of which Antoine discovers that her luggage is marked "R.H." The tragedy recalls *Bérénice:* the consciousness of both partners that their love is at an end, their awareness and their acceptance of the fatality driving them, their self-control, once the passionate explanations have ended. After Rachel leaves the hotel in the early morning, Antoine goes to the wharf to watch the steamer go out. At the end of the paragraph— the end of the affair—Martin du Gard gives to his language a lyricism which, by its rarity, marks the finality and the tragedy of the warmest of human relationships:

> Rachel! She was there, a few hundred meters away, leaning as he was, doubtless, leaning towards him, fixing on him, without seeing him, her eyes blinded by tears; and all their mutilated love, which once again pushed them toward one another, was powerless to procure for them the consolation of a supreme gesture of goodbye. Only the luminous beam of the lighthouse, over Antoine's head, touched with its intermittent caress this mass without a face which, already, was fading again in the mist, carrying away, like a secret, the last and so precarious conjunction of their eyes. (I, 1047-48)

La Belle saison ends with an image of Antoine in the railroad station, exhausted, suffering, waiting for the return train.

II   La Consultation

After the manner of a dramatist, Martin du Gard achieves both concision of time and action and precision of character portrayal in *La Consultation*. The action is chronologically pin-pointed—13 October 1913—and covers an elapsed time of four-teen hours: the afternoon and the evening of one of Antoine's days of consultation. The action is episodic; the range of characters, moreover, is much wider than in previous volumes, and, with their different circumstances, forms a social tableau. Yet there is unity of concern around Antoine, his activity and his preoccupations, and each episode, interesting in itself, is also immediately related to the character of the doctor.

It is an indication of the importance Martin du Gard attributes to medicine that he should make this volume center, not only on Antoine but, more precisely, on his professional activity. Antoine sees himself constantly in the role of doctor. All his values are expressed thereby and he does not know, really, any other self. The results of this monomania are depicted as fortunate ones. "What fine work this is!" he repeats to himself with justification, as he dispenses help, both moral and physical. He has both that satisfaction with oneself which, for Stendhal, was the heart of all morality, and the evidence of others' happiness or well-being for which he is, in part, responsible. Martin du Gard's implication is clearly to give the physical its due: indeed, it seems primary. Antoine speaks more than once of the brute, a priori value of life, to which other values, moral and intellectual, are posterior. In maintaining life, he is working with the most fundamental of all concerns, and finds thereby that his special pride is justified. "He accepted as dogma that medical science was the end of all intellectual effort, and constituted the most certain profit of twenty centuries of groping around in all directions of knowledge, the richest domain open to man's genius" (I, 1130). When, later, this position is qualified (in the *Epilogue*), it will be, not because a rival value has imposed itself in him, but because he will question *all* values including that of life itself.

The incidents of the day involve a score of characters, some of whom have appeared in other circumstances already, and vary from the routine to the tragic. Antoine begins the afternoon by visiting his bed-ridden father who has serious kidney disease and will not recover. This is the prelude of his long agony in *La Mort du père*. Next, he visits, in company with his former professor Dr. Philip, the dying baby daughter of Mme de Fontanin's cousin Nicole, who is now married to a doctor, Héquet. This is the occasion for a portrait of Philip, whom Antoine has so admired that he has consciously modeled some of his behavior on him, and whom he regards nevertheless as an older rival whom he must surpass. Philip, in spite of his rough edges and rather disobliging first impression, is the model of professional integrity; he inspires confidence in everyone.

Nicole Héquet is pregnant again and the husband fears for the unborn child the consequences of Nicole's grief and her sense of guilt. Héquet himself, accustomed to illness and death, cannot reconcile himself to the the suffering of his own child. The double sense of human responsibility (the mother reproaches herself for the illness) and helplessness oppresses the family. A medical assistant tells Antoine that he should give a strong enough dose of narcotic to kill the suffering child. This is the first of three cases during the novel where Antoine will consider euthanasia. This time, he refuses to consent to it and gives to Studler the traditional answers: the doctor has no right to make the judgment of taking life; his only concern is to prolong life. He gives a carefully-measured sedative and leaves. But he is not satisfied with his own answers and, walking in the darkened streets, he argues with himself on the duty of a doctor in his position. During the night the child dies: Antoine will not know whether it was through the normal progress of the disease, whether had had perhaps given too much drug, or whether the assistant had dismissed the nurse and given a fatal injection.

Antoine has several appointments which introduce stories neighboring on the melodramatic. By control of the language, and through Antoine's own attitude of skepticism, reasonableness, and deliberation, Martin du Gard prevents these cases from drawing too much attention away from Antoine. In several cases, humanity prevails over the truth, as with M. Thibault, whom Antoine deceives about the fatal nature of his illness. A drama is adumbrated when Antoine receives the visit of Anne de Battaincourt, her daughter Huguette, and her English governess. Anne, widowed in mysterious circumstances, is now the wife of one of Jacques' school acquaintances. Her daughter has advanced tuberculosis, contracted because of her weak constitution inherited through her father. Anne's visit, however, is not made for the daughter, but because she wants to procure morphine illegally. She tries in vain to use her own wiles and those of the governess to appeal to Antoine. (It should be observed that there is a suggestion of abnormal intimacy between these two women.) Two other episodes introduce into the narrative representatives of *les petites gens*, giving Martin du Gard the chance to reveal his understanding of those who, in the decades before the war, were the laborers and the employees.

For the first time in *Les Thibault*, politics, which will play a role in *La Sorellina* and be crucial in *L'Eté 1914*, appears here, not directly (for Antoine is still indifferent to what is going on in France and in Europe) but through the conversation of one of his patients, Rumelles, attached to the Minister of Foreign Affairs. Rumelles comes to receive treatment for an unmentionable and embarrassing malady. During their conversation, he reveals the realignment of European political forces subsequent to the Entente Cordiale: the rapprochment of Germany and Austria-Hungary, the increased aggressiveness of the Austrians against the Balkan states. He predicts the clash of the French, English, and Russians with the Germans and Austrians, before two or three years. Antoine, who has heard voices of war for some years and who has no great respect for Rumelles' intellect, remains skeptical and turns his attention away from the political question.

Although Antoine's professional life and his deliberations are the central thread of *La Consultation,* a number of allusions and one crucial scene direct our attention to the other Thibaults and reveal what has happened in the family since the summer of *La Belle saison.* The crucial event has been the disappearance of Jacques. Through Antoine's retrospection and an important scene where Gise, too, reflects on what happened, we discover, bit by bit, that Jacques disappeared in November, 1910—three years previously—and that no news has been received from him since.[3] The abundant indications of his instability and dissatisfaction in *La Belle saison* illuminate this event which we see only indirectly but understand without difficulty. M. Thibault believes that Jacques is dead. Antoine worked for over a year on clues that might lead him to his brother; none was successful. Only Gise has remained persuaded that Jacques is alive. That she has special reasons to understand him, and to believe in him, is clear when she recalls the basket of roses that she received from London, without a sender's name, two years before.[4] She believed at the time that this was not only a sign that Jacques was alive but also an admission of his love for her. In *La Belle saison* there was only the briefest suggestion of an interest he might take in her. It is clear now that her own feelings for him were strong and that she had some reason to think that her love might be returned.

After receiving the flowers, Gise, only seventeen, used her ingenuity to persuade Mlle de Waize and M. Thibault that she should learn English in order to prepare herself to earn her living someday as a governess, and spent a summer in England, trying to trace the sender of the flowers. All her efforts were fruitless; but she is planning a return visit. Like Antoine, like M. Thibault, she is a monomaniac, thinking of nothing but her love and ready to sacrifice anything to find Jacques. During these years when they have been the only two young people around the Thibault household, Antoine has developed an inclination for Gise—not a profound love, but a vague need, based on admiration. She is blind to any indications of it, and he is put off when she speaks stubbornly of returning to England. As a man who is used to achieving his goals, he will not long pursue a prey that eludes him. And, since Gise will not reveal to Antoine the secret of her love for Jacques, which is the fount of all her determination, he mistakes her resolution for selfishness and indifference. The misunderstandings within the household, comparable to those that weighed on Jacques, are prolonged.

Although Jacques occupied a central place in *La Belle saison,* the events of the last three years are told retrospectively and obliquely, without his appearing directly at all, and without our having any knowledge other than that of the other characters. This oblique presentation has a number of advantages. It corresponds formally to what Jacques has done physically: he has disappeared. Just as in *Le Pénitencier,* we share here the ignorance of those who speculate about Jacques. He remains for us, as for Gise and Antoine, a mystery, with that shadowy, unknowable quality which characterizes some human beings in particular and which reminds us that Martin du Gard knows that all is not lucid and reasonable in the human spectrum, that the essential being of another escapes us. Furthermore, this prepares the technique of the following volume, that of having us, along with Antoine, rediscover Jacques by something he has written. Meanwhile, the concentration of the novelist's understanding is on Antoine, whose organized professional career will seem to contrast so much with what we will later discover of Jacques' activities. Finally, this limited viewpoint, by which we have only the speculations of Antoine and Gise (and even these are very limited) will enable Martin du Gard to give at a later time, without repetition, Jacques' view of his departure, with the contrasts afforded by the different subjective interpretations.

The volume ends with a professional *examen de conscience* and a series of meditations on morality in which Antoine, for the first time in the novel, formulates his tentative answer to the ethical problem as he sees it. Since this explicit statement of the problem is related to much of the following action of *Les Thibault,* as well as to what we have seen of Antoine so far, it is worthwhile examining. Moreover, it comes strikingly close in points to what we can deduce from the novelist's work and from others' comments on him as his own proposed answer to the question of moral standards and precepts. Antoine is wondering why he refused to approve the proposal of euthanasia. His answer, the respect for life, is only half-satisfactory, for he remembers a story of a two-headed child born in Brittany whom he certainly would be in favor of suppressing; and he had that day told his servant to drown the newborn cats. He wonders whether he has not taken the line of least resistance. His morality has been, generally, to choose the harder of two solutions if otherwise they seem equal. This is not intended as a Nietzschian cultivation of the will (although he quotes Nietzsche's "Man is not a problem, but a solution"); it is rather a practical attitude which has stood him in good stead.

Reflecting further on his choice, he realizes that he does in each case what *he* chooses to do, since he recognizes no moral laws. The notions of good, evil, *ought,* and so on are practical concepts for him which have an empiric reference but refer ultimately only to the customary; he recognizes them as ultilitarian, no more. He decides that his only unfailing principle is: complete liberty of action provided he is lucid. This, he recognizes, is potentially dangerous; one thinks of Gide's *Immoraliste.* But he can admit no other law, only, at the most, a kind of collective morality to which, practically speaking, everyone must subscribe. However, he realizes that his life is organized all the same as if there were some rule he followed. His behavior is moral, even exemplary. But he does not know why. This leads to a double question: Why do I act as I act? and Who am I? It is curious that this latter question, associated earlier with Jacques, reappears in Antoine. He will explore it later in his diary. For the time being he discovers no answer. Although he recognizes a direction in his life—where contradictions are rare—he can find neither psychological nor ethical justification for it.

This stand is to be compared with Martin du Gard's own, which was in part expressed by Gide in his *Journal.* Relating a conversation with Martin du Gard in March, 1927, he noted, "He will not admit that anything can stop man on the inclination of his instincts, except the fear of a policeman God—in whom he does not believe. The foundation of all morality can only be religious, he affirms, and he is surprised and irritated by the disproof which is given to his thesis by the simple manifestations of his own being, so naturally honest and good" (p. 832). Here, as with Antoine, there is an apparent contradiction between a traditional moral behavior and the refusal to recognize traditional foundations of morality. Antoine is thus a means for Martin du Gard to explore the psychology of morality in an atheistic and scientific framework.

In *La Consultation* we see the positivistic Martin du Gard at his best, casting a careful observer's eye on the species of the doctor, examining the principles on which he acts, studying a range of human types. If the characters in the foreground here are not as powerful as those in other volumes—M. Thibault, Jacques, Rachel—it is in part because they are seen here at the common denominator level of the physical; it is also partly because they are to be taken as typical cases more than as individuals. Antoine, through his profession and his commitment to it, dominates the entire volume. The reader acquires here an understanding of him and of his assumptions which illuminates subsequent parts of the novel, and a view of some of the principles of conduct and of valuation which are fundamental to Martin du Gard's interpretation of society and of the individual.

In *La Belle saison* and *La Consultation* Martin du Gard has isolated significant moments in one summer and on a day three years later and has given us, not the whole thread of development of the characters, but stages and high points. This presentation has the advantage of focusing on a limited number of characters at once, of suspending our involvement and then recapturing it with heightened curiosity, and of keeping the dynamics of the novels within workable dimensions, If, on occasions, the situation of a character or characters seems static (as with Jenny in *La Belle saison*), this is only a pause to allow interest to be concentrated elsewhere; with sure skill, Martin du Gard will return to M. Thibault and to Jacques in *La Sorellina*, and to the Fontanins when they once again become closely involved in the lives of the Thibault family.

CHAPTER 6

Les Thibault: La Sorellina and
La Mort du Père

I La Sorellina

LIKE *La Consultation, La Sorellina* presents a nucleus of events, in a very short period of time (about one week), at which several different threads of the plot development come together and are treated through central episodes. Part of the structure is thus chronological, in the narrative time of the main story. Within this structure, however, there is a story-within-a-story: a device which Martin du Gard uses with special effectiveness, for both exposition of plot and revelation of character through psychologically charged symbols. Jacques, who is unseen in the first part of the volume, is really nevertheless at the center of it. His story, "La Sorellina," which Antoine reads, is the central discovery and leads to all the subsequent events of the volume. By this story Jacques' consciousness radiates through Antoine's thoughts, dictates his actions, and yet reaches the reader directly. Like the whole of *Les Thibault*, this story-within-a-story is the attempt of the imaginary author, Jacques, and the real author, Martin du Gard, to reach an inner truth through imagination, using literary conventions and linguistic symbols.

The volume opens with M. Thibault. Although Antoine is a principal actor here, the determining will is, to some extent, M. Thibault's, and it is suitable that the author show him in the first scenes, irascible, tyrannical, occupied with himself and with others' opinions of him. Perhaps it is incorrect to speak of *will*, however: it is his condition, unwilled but undergone by him, which is an essential fact. For M. Thibault is seriously ill—less so than he proclaims to others during the moments of self-edification during which he preaches resignation and wishes to give the example of a noble death; more so than he admits to himself, or than Antoine lets him know. After an operation, convalescence, and a relapse, his system is gravely undermined, and Antoine knows that he will die shortly, probably of uremic poisoning. Meanwhile, he pontificates from his bed, comforted by the fiction—carefully maintained by Antoine—that his atrocious sufferings are caused by the medication which is acting. Since M. Chasle is not a fully developed consciousness but only a puppet character, when we see M. Thibault alone with him we see him alone—acting out a role for himself, prey to fears, doubts, and nightmares, obsessed with his image and sententiously giving advice.

The author gives M. Thibault one particularly good chance for playing his role. Having persuaded himself, in pretending, that he will shortly die, he assembles the household around him to distribute his blessings and express his last wishes. The farewell is painful in its ironies: M. Thibault not really believing in his death; M. Chasle, certain that his protector will be gone, and worrying about his own future; the more innocent of the females taken in, but not the nurse; and Antoine, realizing that death is closer, and will be far more painful, than his father recognizes.

During these scenes, there is no mention of Jacques. M. Thibault has continually insisted that Jacques killed himself; Antoine has never been so persuaded. The following day, Antoine finds in the mail a letter for Jacques, from a professor at the Ecole Normale, congratulating Jacques on a story that has just appeared. Antoine is moved by the realization that his brother is indeed alive. With his usual speed of action, he conceives a plan for visiting the professor, Jalicourt, and discovering all he can about Jacques, not so that he may interfere with his life, but so that he can tell him of their father's serious condition.

The novel has an element of mystery as Antoine tries to piece together what Jalicourt tells him of Jacques. The professor received a copy of the story, "La Sorellina," published in a review at Geneva, signed "Jack Baulthy." It was inscribed with an illusion to the two faces of love. Jalicourt tells how Jacques came to see him, about three years before (just at the time he disappeared, and when Antoine himself was with Rachel at Le Havre), to ask his advice: should he enter the Ecole Normale, or choose another road, less certain? A few days later, Jalicourt had received from Jacques a hand-written copy of a poem of Whitman. This was the last news until the arrival of the review.

In *Souvenirs* (I, xcv) Martin du Gard tells how the story-within-a-story technique of telling the reader the sentimental reasons for Jacques' departure seemed skillful to him, but how he labored for months to construct the story. The fact is a revealing one: he felt that it was necessary to write the whole text as Jacques would, although Antoine reads carefully only crucial portions of it, skipping over descriptions; this would, the novelist thought, give it the character of authenticity. Moreover, he wanted the style to be different from his own and indicative of Jacques' passionate nature. Gide suggested that the labor of composing the whole thing was useless, but Martin du Gard went ahead with his plan. Later, he realized that Gide had been right. It is true that the extracts one reads are convincing; but one reads them for the information and the light shed on Jacques, not for the style. The extreme conscientiousness of craft, which Martin du Gard felt and attributed to Antoine in his profession, was here out of proportion with the result obtained.

Antoine goes to a Latin Quarter cafe to read the story. From among the short, impressionistic sentences, he gleans names and bits of description, centered around an Italian family and including Giuseppe, an obvious transposition of Jacques himself. At first , however, he discovers nothing relevant to Jacques' departure and little indication of what he might be doing and thinking at present. Jacques remains for him, as he told Jalicourt, "Violent and restless, I dare not say: a visionary" (I, 1165). Suddenly, through a piece of description he recognizes the Fontanins' house at Maisons-Lafitte, and then realizes that the Protestant Powell family represents the Fontanins, and that the enigmatic Sybil Powell is Jenny. Giuseppe's hatred for his father, his revolt and his scorn, must be the sentiments that were Jacques' at the time he was at Maisons-Lafitte, and perhaps even now. Humberto, the elder brother who did not understand him, is Antoine, and Annetta, the "sorellina," is Gise. As Antoine reads on feverishly, he expresses his reactions. Thus we do not have the story itself but the fragmented story as interpreted by Antoine.

Jacques' prose is choppy, and he gives no explanation of his characters' actions. These follow one another, abruptly, not illuminated by Giuseppe's thoughts but reflected through his own consciousness. Jacques has never seen, it would appear, any drama but his own. He has a narrowly egotistical vision. Through subtle indications, it is clear the Giuseppe has been in love with Sybil, but that this love, though accepted by her, has found no expression. Her coldness and her morbid fear of close contact, of giving herself, certainly recall Jenny at Maisons-Lafitte. Then, when the little sister Annetta returns from her convent school, Giuseppe's sensibility finds an outlet. They live in an intimacy based on their childhood memories but actually reaching much farther. Yet Giuseppe does not seem to be aware of it. In an extremely inhibited scene, Giuseppe asks Sybil to be his for life; she silently consents. Later, he takes his sister to visit the Powells (which his father has forbidden), announces to her that he loves Sybil, and causes such a strong reaction that he becomes aware of his sister's love for him. There follows a distinctly incestuous scene in which the two discover their common physical passion which, one may assume, is consummated. Upon returning to their father's villa, they are confronted by him, in a rage. Giuseppe tells of the visit to the English family; he and his father quarrel bitterly with what Antoine may suppose is an accurate transcription of the curses M. Thibault must have hurled at his son when the latter announced that he was involved with the Fontanins. The son's threat to kill himself explains M. Thibault's obsession with the hypothesis of suicide. Giuseppe decides that, not being able to have both loves, the pure and the sensual, he will leave without either, cutting all bridges, committing himself to a new life.

Appalled by the suggestion that Jacques and Gise have had a passionate relationship and recognizing the accuracy of the portrait of the Fontanins and M. Thibault, Antoine is forced to accept the story as throwing light on Jacques' departure and as giving, perhaps, the total secret of his brother. Jacques' relationship with Gise would not have been strictly incestuous, but it gives to Antoine a conception of Gise so different from the timid and modest girl he had known that his own vanity is wounded. Whatever the exact truth, much is illuminated retrospectively by the story. More important, he believes he can trace Jacques. Within three days a private agent brings him the information that Jacques is living in Lausanne and working as a journalist. Antoine resolves to go to appeal that he return to see his father.

Arriving in Lausanne, Antoine goes directly to Jacques' boarding house and surprises him at his breakfast. After a moment of revolt and anger, Jacques becomes docile when he learns that their father is dying, and he consents, without enthusiasm but as though accepting the inevitable, to return temporarily to Paris. The first scenes are written with limited omniscience, from Antoine's point of view. The secret internal logic of Jacques has been central to the story since *Le Cahier gris,* and it has underlain the recent parts. It would be impossible to elucidate this logic from the exterior only; and Martin du Gard must have felt that it was time to bring it directly into the scene, if not wholly, at least sufficiently to satisfy some of the reader's curiosity and illuminate Jacques' disappearance. Moreover, Jacques will be the chief actor in most of *L'Eté 1914,* and his political convictions, which inspire his action, can only be understood against the background of his character and his development since leaving his family.

Jacques gives Antoine occasional insights into himself but does not develop them—through fear of committing himself, of opening himself to appeals of a duty which he does not recognize. Moreover, a certain *pudeur* still obtains between the brothers. Through Jacques' thoughts, we see that he has made a tenable life in Lausanne with his writing, journalism, and political activities. Though he does not consider that a true happiness is possible for him at all, he has created at least a *modus vivendi* and is morbidly afraid of contact with the past or invasions of his privacy.

One important insight which comes of their limited discussion concerns Gise. Curious to know Antoine's impression of "La Sorellina," Jacques questions him and is amazed to learn that Antoine interprets the entire story, with its incestuous love and the symbol of red roses (one remembers the roses that Gise received from London) as an accurate transcription of what happened in the summer at Maisons-Lafitte. Jacques assures him that there was no passionate relationship with Gise. Yet he reflects on the memory he has of one sensuous kiss, of his realization of her love for him, of his own interest in the cold Jenny—and finally reveals to Antoine that he and his father did quarrel over the Fontanins, his father cursing him, he threatening to kill himself. This is Martin du Gard's technique of correction: bringing to bear at a later time an important qualification to what we have supposed, as well as fulfillment of plot suggestions.[1] Truth is multi-faceted and subjective, but instead of stating this, the novelist shows it by a gradual revelation of "truth" through a change of the angle of vision.

In the same way, Jacques relates his last visit with Jalicourt, giving a different account from Jalicourt's. Jacques had not already determined to leave school in Paris when he went to visit the professor; it was the latter's attitude, negative and then embarrassingly honest, which gave Jacques the final realization that he must cut all his ties with the past and with academic education. In a passage which recalls Nietzsche's (and Gide's) attacks on culture, he had exclaimed, "I explained to him everything! That I felt in myself a force, something intimate, central, which is mine, which exists! That, for years, every effort towards culture had almost always been exercized to the detriment of this profound value. That I had aversion for studies, schools, erudition . . . and that this horror had the violence of an instinct of defense, of preservation!" (I, 1234). Looking forward to an existentialist view, he had added, "I hate classifiers . . . On the pretext of classifying you, they limit you, they gnaw you . . ." (I, 1235).

The last pages of *La Sorellina* show Jacques and Antoine returning to Paris, exhausted, each a prey to his own thoughts. Their common destination only accentuates the separation between them. Martin du Gard excells in the portrayal of anguish—the low, unverbalized anguish of men alienated from each other and from themselves. Truly, Jacques does not seem to be entirely *present*. In *La Mort du père*, he will think of the world as being strange, a stranger to him (I, 1279); here, he is a stranger to his own mind. The volume closes with Jacques obstinately closing his eyes, pretending to sleep.

II La Mort du père

This volume, tied closely to the preceding one by time and subject matter, begins with a flashback: we see Mlle de Waize on the evening when Antoine has left for Lausanne, occupied at the same task she was doing when Antoine came to tell her goodbye. The first two chapters are focussed on M. Thibault. Physical existence and suffering have entirely taken him over; and the novelist concentrates with considerable, perhaps excessive, detail on the medical aspects of his agony. This description of physical deterioration and death is made for the sake of authenticity or realism; it is also clear that this process of dying holds for the author considerable importance—not only the extinction of consciousness but the previous humiliation of physical decay. As in *Jean Barois,* death appears as a central fact of existence, perhaps *the* central fact, not only a sociological fact and a physical one, but an existential reality. As with certain authors of the following generation—Malraux and Sartre in particular—men in Martin du Gard's novels appear as creatures-for-death. "Ultimately," says Antoine, "only death exists: it refutes everything, goes beyond everything . . . absurdly! " (I, 1305). It is to be noticed that during these chapters Martin du Gard speaks more frequently than usual in the authorial voice, giving generalizations and comments on the problem of death (e.g. I, 1253).

As with Barois, the question of death is for M. Thibault complicated by the religious problem. Maintaining his objective tone, the author shows both the failure and the success of religious belief at the moment of agony. Failure: for, when Abbé Vécard first comes to administer rites and pray the prayers for the dying, M. Thibault repulses him brutally, saying that his consolations have nothing to do with the fact that he is dying and wants to live; then he blasphemes against God who is either non-existent or cruel, being the cause of this suffering and of the imminent extinction. The resignation which the abbé preaches has no relationship with the terror M. Thibault feels and with his resentment at having his life taken away from him, at being powerless to control himself and others. Moreover, M. Thibault is extremely lucid and cannot swallow the hollow assurances of the abbé that he has led a charitable, noble life: in a moment of truth, he admits to himself that all his acts have been motivated by vanity and self-interest, that he wanted the praise of men rather than the glory of God. Yet the rites and the words of the priest ultimately have their efficacity on the psychological plane. The novelist shows the priest applying the formulas of consolation and of preparation over and over, almost like a litany, until they finally have a soothing effect on M. Thibault and he can once again abandon himself to what is in Martin du Gard's eyes a myth. "These sacred words must have been in themselves very effective, after centuries of experience they must have been strictly appropriate to the fears of agony, in order to act so quickly, so directly, on so much terror, on such a rebellion" (I, 1262). Thus Martin du Gard explains the role of religion which is a compendium of empirically perfected formulas for acting upon the human imagination.

As Antoine and Jacques arrive in Paris, the attention is on Jacques more than on Antoine, for his return is not only a visit to a dying father but also an encounter with his past—with Mlle de Waize, with Gise who returns from England, with his complex of feelings towards his father. We see Jacques in part through his own thoughts, as he broods alone; in part through his short conversations with Antoine and with Gise (who finds Jacques a stranger, irremediably lost to her) and through his attitude in the sickroom. Along with this psychological interest, there is continued attention on the death agony of M. Thibault. He is in the last stages of uremia: his kidney functions scarcely at all. But as long as it continues to revive from time to time, his life will be prolonged. Meanwhile, he is prey to horrible convulsive attacks. Antoine and the other doctor, Thérivier, know that M. Thibault cannot possibly recover. After one particularly severe attack, during which M. Thibault struggles like a great wild animal, Jacques asks his brother whether something cannot be done. He answers that there *is* something— the radical gesture which is the permanent suppression of suffering. Without discussion, the two brothers mutually consent to euthanasia, and during a moment when the nurses are away, Antoine gives his father the fatal dose of morphine which at long last brings calm to the features and the limbs of the ravaged body. As when the narrator's grandmother dies in *Le Côté de Guermantes,* death brings to M. Thibault a new fulfillment: "Raised on the pillow, suddenly taller, in the full light, M. Thibault, with the knots of the handkerchief tied around his chin standing out like horns on his head, had taken on the mysterious and theatrical appearance of a legendary character" (I, 1301). This awesome picture is qualified by the ridiculous choir of Mlle de Waize and the maids, reciting litanies for the dead in a singsong voice.

Antoine reflects on the meaning of death. He can look at it both from an existential viewpoint and a scientific one. In a natural perspective, life goes on, lives after lives, ad infinitum, and there is no *néant*. But for a particular being, for a particular consciousness, there *is* extinction; and the problem of *how* and *why* persists. These views will return in Antoine's diary in the *Epilogue.* As for the question of euthanasia, he dismisses what he has done with a clear conscience, knowing that he has acted for the welfare of his father as well as of those around him who had to endure his suffering; knowing that he would not raise what he did to the level of a general maxim, and yet that he was justified, ethics being a question of the specific rather than the general. It is not until Héquet, the doctor who lost his infant daughter, comes to give him his commiseration that he realizes that he has taken a new departure, and that, by this action, he is somehow forever changed.

At the graveside ceremonies for his father, before observing that his death marks the end of an era, Antoine thinks to himself, "One succeeds in understanding a man only after his death. As long as a being lives, all the things which he can still accomplish, and of which one is ignorant, constitute unknowns which distort calculations. Death arrests finally the contours . . ." (I, 1357). This reflection, which has a Sartrian ring, also illuminates the chapter in which Antoine goes through his father's papers and discovers a man quite different from the one which he—and the reader—knew. Martin du Gard's imaginative insight into human beings is rarely so well revealed as here. For instance, Antoine reads the old letters from his father to his mother and discovers a tender, sentimental lover as well as a paternalistic and patronizing man. In his innumerable notebooks, Antoine finds indications of the effort which M. Thibault had to make to be charitable, the discipline he exercised on himself to be what to his sons always seemed like his natural self. Signs of anguish, of pride and disgust with pride, of temptation and perhaps even of sin fill the notebooks as much as statements of self-satisfaction. M. Thibault kept a sheet in which he called Jacques rebellious and perverse; but he also kept letters from both his sons and from Gise, and revealed at times what Antoine interprets as a character like Jacques' own, difficult and unhappy. M. Thibault was both much more than what his son suspected—with resources of understanding and sensibility—and much less than the world thought—since his piety is contradicted by egoism and doubt. The theme of fathers and sons is developed here in a new way, as Antoine realizes that he and his father could have loved and understood each other, had each made the effort, instead of remaining strangers hidden behind masks; but that it is now forever too late.

Gise comes to have an explanation with Jacques, to reveal her own love and ascertain his sentiments. Her distress evokes for a moment in him a feeling of sympathy, which is, however, physical attraction rather than true pity. He then is so disgusted with his momentary attraction (which recalls to him their kiss, three years ago, and all its implications) that he pushes her away. Realizing that she is fated to love him (an indication which looks forward to the *Epilogue*) but not be loved by him, she leaves before further words of alienation can be pronounced. In this scene, as in previous ones with Jenny, Jacques appears clearly as a Puritan. The simple acceptance of physical life which has been easy for Antoine but was probably impossible for their father is likewise impossible for Jacques. There is no reason other than self-imposed inhibitions why he should scorn the passionate feeling of Gise and forbid himself to be drawn to her. It is not a question of morals—for he does not reason that it is unfair to caress Gise if he will not marry her—but a refusal to accept himself and to admit to anyone else's impinging upon him, even by physical desire.

He reappears in a short episode when he takes the train to Crouy to see his father's grave, after the ceremonies, in which he did not participate. His ambiguous feelings about his dead father—over whom he weeps sentimentally for an instant, although he hates him also and would hate him if he were still alive—reflect onto his feelings about himself: a fundamental irreconciliation to his own life, to his sentiments, his past, his demands, and the demands of the world on him. He is prey to an existentialist anguish, provoked by reflection on his father's death but centered on himself. Given the fact of death—and because of his own character—nothing seems worthwhile to him. This is in part what Camus would later call the discovery of the absurd, and the consequent problem of valuation. In the last chapter of *La Mort du père*, Antoine and Abbé Vécard reintroduce the problem of values. Here, Jacques muses, as he had earlier, on the nothingness of life. "Why want? What to hope? All existence is derisory. Nothing, absolutely nothing, is worthwhile—as soon as one knows death" (I, 1367). He longs to escape—from himself, from life—but that escape could only be death. He considers suicide as an idea, abstract but attractive, and has fantasies of destroying Crouy by fire. These indications prepare his final self-willed destruction in *L'Eté 1914*. Few aspects of *Les Thibault* are so disquietingly modern as this study of self-depreciation and nihilism.

Martin du Gard introduces, by means of an affectionate letter from Daniel to Jacques, information on the Fontanins. There follows a closing dialogue on religious belief between Antoine and Abbé Vécard, who are returning by train from Crouy. Themes familiar to readers of *Jean Barois* reappear here, with the arguments condensed and refined. The priest argues well—better than Joziers, certainly—so that one cannot accuse the author of deliberate unfairness. Antoine, too, has a more systematic view of his own atheism than Jean did, for Jean's was colored by his own painful liberation from belief, whereas Antoine came to his disbelief, as he says, naturally, without any rebellion. Moreover, Antoine's mind is more ample than Jean's. The result is an excellent résumé of the arguments for and against Christian belief, the first against the background of an enlightened, postmodernistic faith, the second from a scientific view of the world with doubt as the point of departure. Neither man will, of course, sway the other. The discussion is nevertheless of use to Antoine, for he looks at his own disbelief critically and, exceptionally, formulates some of his positions. He again recognizes the problem raised by the disparity between his own actions, based on a kind of professional *Il faut,* and his professed belief that *nothing* is necessary and that there is no justifiable imperative. He even comes to admit to the priest, not that he wishes to believe, but that he would be happy to be able to accept some kind of consolation at death, since death without hope is, he has seen, a dreadful, not an admirable, spectacle. This is a wish which, ironically, wil not be realized.

The reasons which Antoine gives for his disbelief are not only close to those professed by Jean Barois; they recall the statements Martin du Gard made about his own absence of faith. The passage can thus be taken as a credo of the author. While this need not be true in every particular, it is surely accurate to observe the parallels in thought and to surmise that Martin du Gard put much of himself directly into this episode. Antoine quotes a statement which a priest made to him once: "Perhaps you do not have the religious sense." This seems borne out by his own declarations that he had no religious crisis and was never religiously sensitive as a child, that his need to understand is greater than his need to believe, that "my atheism was formed at the same time as my mind," and that "my intelligence, my will, my character developed outside of religion" (I, 1377, 1386-87).[2] When formulated in intellectual terms, his arguments against belief in God are based on a scientific view that God is not demonstrable, visible, or probable, and that the world seems undirected by Providence, as likely without organization as with, a simple series of causes and effects.[3] However, Antoine's objections (like the views of the priest) are ultimately less intellectual than personal: as he says, he simply does not believe and feels no appeal to belief within him. This is Antoine's—and, presumably—Martin du Gard's final word on the attraction and acceptability of faith. Later, Antoine's attention will be turned, not to the possibility of belief in God, but, as Malraux said, to the possibility of belief in man.

CHAPTER 7

L'Eté 1914

I Characteristics and Structure

TOGETHER with the subsequent *Epilogue*, *L'Eté 1914* forms roughly one half of *Les Thibault*; yet its chronological concentration is intense, since all of the action takes place between June 28 and August 10. Like previous crucial episodes, only on a vaster scale, it is a dramatic moment—the climax to which all else has been preparation. This dramatic moment involves all the chief characters and includes some momentous events in their personal lives; but, more important, it places their destinies against the background of a European crisis and, ultimately, shows that there is no longer, in the twentieth century, a uniquely personal destiny, protected and self-determined. The understanding that Martin du Gard had of contemporary man's political destiny—his involvement, willing or not, in the economic and military dilemmas of a whole world—and his recognition that the European war of 1914 was the decisive proof of this involvement, made him raise the historical backdrop to the level of a principal action, and develop the characters' lives in light of this action. This is, of course, an opportunity for considerable historical and dramatic irony, since the author sees, as most of the characters do not see, by what prolonged destruction the summer of 1914 is to be followed and what effect it will have on their lives. The reader does not yet know the particulars of the latter; but he is aware throughout the volume of the impending disaster, and of the tragic coloration it gives to the simplest of gestures and projects.

It has been argued that this invasion of the action of the novel by political and social concerns forms a structural rupture with preceding parts and creates finally a disequilibrium of the whole.[1] While it cannot be denied that there is a change in tone and in subject matter, it seems like prejudgment to assert that this unbalances the whole novel. Like a biographical novel or *Bildüngsroman,* and a historical novel, *Les Thibault,* partaking of both genres, has a subject matter which is inherently capable of evolution, not only along a foreseen line but along new lines. The maturity of the characters is not of the same order as their youth; the novelist has the choice of stopping (as Alain-Fournier did in *Le Grand Meaulnes*), or of opening his analysis to new perspectives, as Proust did. Similarly, once one accepts the datum that Martin du Gard is portraying the bourgeoisie in France before and at the time of the World War I, one must accept the impingement of history on this social class and on the novel. The novelist could, it is true, have kept this historical element to a minimum; but such would have been a deliberate ignoring of the force with which the political fact struck sensitive young bourgeois like Jacques Thibault, and it would not have been in keeping with Martin du Gard's attempt to give a comprehensive view of a generation.

It can still be objected that there is too much ideological material in the book. France in the summer of 1914 could have been portrayed without lengthy accounts of socialist thought. One can answer this only by suggesting that, for Martin du Gard, this was an essential, not an incidental, element of Europe in 1914; that he wanted to create a counterpoise to the preponderantly bourgeois point of view throughout the novel; and that his character Jacques, who has finally come into his own as a socialist writer and leader, is to be understood in function of these ideas. The ideological element of *L'Eté 1914* throws light on all the preceding parts and qualifies that bourgeois order of which M. Thibault was an epitome; it is an essential element of the total vision of *Les Thibault;* and, if there is apparently a new point of departure in the volume, it is a development, not a contradiction, of what precedes.

Because *L'Eté 1914* is, in fact, a second version of the continuation of *Les Thibault,* since the novelist burnt virtually all of *L'Appareillage,* saving only a few pages concerning Jenny and Jacques, commentators can support their criticism of the disparity between the first and second halves of *Les Thibault.* Martin du Gard has explained his decision: a realization that he could not pursue the entire project, as he had foreseen it, without writing more than a dozen additional volumes; a recognition that the novel as he had planned it would be purely psychological (I, xcvi). (He does not state explicitly that this "purely psychological" nature dissatisfied him; nevertheless, when one considers the changes he introduced, it is apparent that his reflection led him to want to enlarge the perspective of his novel.) After discarding *L'Appareillage* and writing *Un Taciturne,* he prepared his notes for *L'Eté 1914* and the *Epilogue* by the end of 1933 and composed them in the following years. It can be suggested that the political situation in Europe in the early '30s encouraged him to modify his original plan and make of his character study a political drama as well.

The action of the eighty-five chapters of *L'Eté 1914* (labeled in the table of contents by their dates) takes place in a number of different cities, chiefly Geneva and Paris, and is centered around several principal events: first, Jacques' activity in Geneva among his socialist friends; his trip to Paris; the suicide of Jérôme de Fontanin; Jacques' political activities, aimed at raising working-class sentiment against the war; his reconciliation with Jenny; Antoine's mobilization; and Jacques' return to Geneva. Though these events form nuclei of action, there is also considerable simultaneity of action, as one follows Antoine in one involvement and Jacques in another. The effect is a feeling of precipitation—entirely appropriate in the month before the war breaks out, when Jacques at least realizes that Europe is on the brink of disaster. The invasion of the outside world— of history—is progressive, until at the end of the volume even Antoine is caught up in the events which he had deliberately chosen to ignore. Simultaneous dramas, even secret ones, and the sure, terrifying march of time toward the war—this is the action of *L'Eté 1914.*

II *Jacques in Geneva (Chapters I-XII)*

The first twelve chapters of *L'Eté 1914* are an ideological exposition and a portrait of Jacques, much more than a series of incidents. Jacques, who has been shadowy in most of the novel and who has been seen obliquely more often than directly, in spite of his importance, here appears at the center, both as actor and as reflecting consciousness. Through the interaction between him and his entourage at Geneva, Martin du Gard gives an idea of his character as it is now formed, of his beliefs, and of the range of socialist views among all the expatriates there. This is, indeed, a *livre à idées*, though not a *livre à thèse*.

Jacques and his fellows appear scenically with a minimum of exposition, in a number of different episodes, most of which happen one day which, it turns out, is the 28th of June, the date on which the Austrian archduke was assassinated by a Serbian nationalist at Sarajevo. We see Jacques involved in a socialist club, Le Local—in which an important role is played by an older man, Meynestrel, called "The Pilot," and his woman companion, Alfreda. There is a whole range of socialist types here—from the methodical and patriotic Germans, through the passionate Italian who worships Mussolini, the idol of every socialist in Italy (Martin du Gard must have savored the irony of this admiration), through the brutal Mithoerg and the more reflective Jacques. Through their conversation, the author lets us see that some of the men are from working-class backgrounds. Some are passionately international; others, like Jacques and the Belgian Vanheede, believe in the cause of international peace and socialism but find it chimeric to propose disestablishing all national boundaries and concerns. As the discussions develop (recalling by their form the ideological conversations and the camaraderie in *Devenir!* and *Jean Barois*), we see not only the types of pre-World War I socialists but the range of ideas, from opportunism to patriotism to purism; from the belief in violence and class-war as the only revolutionary tools, through "reformism." Following a recurring pattern, there is perpetual argument on the real meaning of the revolution. Each interpretation has its adherents, and all accuse their opponents of misunderstanding or betraying the revolution.

Jacques is somewhat to the right of center. He is attacked by some of his fellows as an intellectual—a thinker who has come to the party by choice rather than necessity. (One recognizes here a criticism familiar to readers of Sartre's novels.) This attack is certainly justified in part. For one thing, Jacques is not certain of his own place in the revolutionary movement. It is important to note that even here, when he believes in the cause and is willing to work for it, he is not entirely at home; he is alienated. He classifies partisans of the revolution into three groups—apostles (those who subscribe to an ideal), technicians, and leaders. Though he is closest to the apostles, he cannot count himself as one of them; he has an ideal but does not believe in it blindly. Belonging in part to all three of these groups, he is situated at the delicate intersection of thinking out and carrying out.

Furthermore, he has certain reservations about revolutionary doctrine. Since he looks beyond the revolution itself, he sees the difficulties inherent in what Malraux calls in *Man's Hope* "organizing the Apocalypse." He may sense that, as Sébastian Faure wrote, "Every revolution ends in the reappearance of a new ruling class."[2] He accepts Marx's theses on the self-condemnation of capitalism, the injustice of the bourgeoisie, and the possibility of a non-profit society. But he does not readily admit with Marx that man is infinitely changeable, a creature only of his social system. Whereas Le Pilote says, in a Marxist and pre-existentialist vision, "Humanity which is rising up with us is beginning a prodigious climb, which will modify, for centuries, not only the condition of man with respect to man, but . . . man himself—even in what he believes to be his instincts!" (II, 78), Jacques wonders whether there is not an eternal man, for whom Utopias are unrealizable. Some of the values for which he is fighting are, he realizes, a legacy from the European humanistic heritage: particularly the notion of the human personality, the individual. He has true sympathy for the proletariat. But the doctrine of class-warfare, with its implied violence, is inimical to him. And he is particularly wary of the axiom that the end justifies the means, fearing that if man compromises himself for an end, the whole man for whom the end is won will be destroyed. As Camus in *The Rebel* and Malraux have pointed out, Justice, by its inherent nature, cannot be achieved unjustly. Likewise, Jacques is unwilling to forgo the sense of nationality. "Condemn this nationalism, to be sure! But must one . . . reject at the same time the feeling for the homeland? this human reality, as it were physical, carnal? . . . Man can expatriate himself, but he cannot *depatriate* himself" (II, 18-19). In short, as the author says, Jacques "did not manage to accept the systematic and radical suppression of the bourgeois culture with which he still felt penetrated" (II, 35).

Against this background, the assassination of the archduke has enormous repercussions. To those who have been observing both the rising nationalist sentiment in Germany and the movement of Panslavism, as well as the French rearmament, the event which gives a pretext to Austria-Hungary to seek revenge and solidify her alliance with Germany is momentous. Jacques is sent by Meynestrel to Austria to contact members of the socialist party and take the pulse of the situation. The reader does not witness these scenes directly but hears them reported when Jacques returns on 12 July and gives a long exposition of the background of the assassination. The group discusses the measures to be taken. This is the occasion for Martin du Gard to develop further an assessment of the European political situation. Jacques' consciousness is again at the center of things, but the political facts count for more than his reflection of them. Attitudes vary, from the Englishman Patterson's naive belief that war will not break out, to Jacques' advocacy of the general strike, to Meynestrel's skepticism about either preventing war or using it as a springboard to the revolution. Meynestrel does not express his discouragement to the group, but waits to tell to Alfreda only that he believes the war is coming too soon because the socialist parties of Europe are not consolidated enough to turn it into a general revolution. The closing note of this section is one of disappointment and anguish.

III   Sunday, July 19 (Chapters XIII-XXIII)

Eleven chapters develop the different incidents which take place in Paris on Sunday, July 19, after Jacques has arrived on a mission. It is the day on which Jérôme de Fontanin shoots himself in the head and agonizes throughout the night. Here the foreground is occupied by the personal dramas of Antoine (who is in the midst of a liaison with Anne de Battaincourt) and of the Fontanins. But the political drama is not out of sight, since a number of pages are devoted to a long argument between Jacques and Antoine on the subject of socialism and the looming war.

Rather than explaining how Anne de Battaincourt (who had obviously been interested in Antoine) managed to enter his life, Martin du Gard presents their liaison as a *fait accompli*. Like Rachel, she is one of the "abominable women" of Baudelaire, who live for their pleasure and whose physical presence secretes an undefinable malaise. She is less sympathetic to the reader than Rachel, for she is closer to criminal than victim, since it is rumored that she poisoned her first husband whom she had married for his money, and since she obviously mistreats her present husband. She is vain, superficial, and without the qualities of heart and understanding which Rachel had.

Jacques stops at his father's house, which Antoine has had redesigned to accommodate his offices and research laboratories. This is an occasion for lengthy discussions between them which present Antoine's character, Jacques' views, and the political situation. Antoine believes that what is happening is merely a local quarrel between Austria and Serbia; and even when Jacques tries to persuade him that the possibility of a generalized European conflict is very great, Antoine refuses to let it disturb him, insisting that it is not his business. There is in Antoine a definite lack of political consciousness; there is also a certain wisdom in his devotion to his profession with its immediate utility, at the expense of a wider social concern. If his naive belief that the reality of political and diplomatic maneuvers is mirrored in the language of speeches and treaties is typical of intellectuals of his time, it reveals how far they were from the political skepticism of later generations (II, 130).

When Jacques raises the subject of capitalism, Antoine answers less as a professional man than as a member of the powerful bourgeoisie, expressing vested interests and taking as a principle that there must be workers and there must be a moneyed aristocracy. Neither arguments appealing to moral values (Jacques, following Marx, sees that capitalism has eroded real values and alienated man from himself) nor arguments directed at practical difficulties (the problematic nature of an economy based on infinitely-expandable markets and increasing monopolies) move Antoine to admit that capitalism is not a fair and workable system, relatively speaking—which, in his eyes, is all one can hope for.

[122]

To support his counter-arguments, Antoine has recourse to the notion that human nature does not change and will always require the profit motive and a caste of leaders in order to produce for modern society. Here, he touches on the one weak point in Jacques' presentation. For Jacques is himself skeptical concerning the success of the revolution. (This skepticism is akin to doubts underlying much of Martin du Gard's fiction.) "His pity for men was infinite; he devoted all the love of his heart to them; but no matter what he did . . . no matter how he repeated with fervent conviction the doctrinal formulas, he remained skeptical concerning the moral possibilities of men. . . . He did not believe . . . in the infallibility of this dogma: the spiritual progress of man" (II, 164). (It is pertinent to remember here Martin du Gard's accusation of human nature in *Vieille France* and other works.) Here, Jacques is much closer to Antoine than he would like to admit. But whereas for Antoine, this is a fundamental view which is not contradicted by his daily efforts to increase the physical well-being of men, for Jacques the view is a denial of his aspirations, and it undermines what he does. His consciousness here is truly tragic.

The remainder of the action on July 19 surrounds Jérôme de Fontanin who, caught embezzling business funds and involved in debts and love affairs, has finally shot himself. At the clinic where Jérôme lies in a coma, Jenny sees Jacques for the first time in four years. It is a multi-faceted encounter: Mme de Fontanin seeing her husband, who had caused her so much misery, now punished by his own hand; Jenny facing the boy whose love she had had to smother in her heart; Jacques facing the girl whose image had caused him to quarrel with his father and at the same time leave her.

A few days later, even Daniel and Nicole Héquet appear. Daniel too has not seen Jacques since the summer at Maisons-Lafitte. He tries to renew their intimacy but fails before the mute denials of Jacques. The latter is making what could be called in Sartrian terms an existentialist choice: the choice to deny himself and his past and to be a stranger. Though Daniel does have different views of women and politics from those of Jacques, his desire to find a common terrain of understanding is manifest, and his intuition is not so narrow that it would be impossible. But Jacques refuses him access and takes refuge in a vision of Daniel killed on the Eastern Front (he has in fact been assigned to a garrison in the East). When Nicole Héquet arrives later, for the funeral, it is the first time that she and Daniel have talked for some years. She, like the others, relives much of the past on the occasion of this death, and compares the bitterness of the present with her hopes in earlier years. Even the bizarre Christian Scientist, Pastor Gregory, reappears, to affirm in the midst of all this anguish (only Antoine, busy with his professional work, feels any contentment) that evil and suffering do not exist.

Jenny's precarious equilibrium is entirely broken by the sight of Jacques. She had managed a kind of contentment because she had given up all hope of seeing him again. Now she feels the hope and despair well up in her again. This disappointed love takes the not-uncommon form of hate: she refuses to look Jacques in the face, avoids him, and tells her mother that she hates him. Jacques' attraction towards her is similarly felt as repulsion. He resents the memories which she evokes and hates in himself the man who was sensitive to her.

IV   *Monday, July 20-Saturday, July 25*
(Chapters XXIV-XXXVIII)

During this week the action is centered on Jacques, on the Fontanins (Jérôme finally dies and is buried), and on the political situation, increasingly grave. Chapters dealing with the personal dramas of the characters alternate with those in which politics is at the forefront, until at the end of this part, Jacques finds himself reflecting that his personal destiny—his love for Jenny—and the possibility of war are tragically tied together.

As Gaëtan Picon has remarked, Martin du Gard shows in these chapters of *L'Eté 1914* which deal with the diplomatic maneuvering preceding the war his extraordinary command of facts and his ability to recreate a complex political situation in which he was not involved. Picon speaks of the "extraordinary impression of *choses vues*" which is the fruit of a patient documentation.[3] As happens in a contemporary political situation, one learns *gradually* about the developments between Austria and Serbia and of their repercussions elsewhere; Martin du

Gard does not intervene to foresee their ultimate result but lets us instead witness the march of events and their reflection in the newspapers. Departing from the procedure of *Jean Barois,* he does not insert lengthy extracts from the press but condenses the news as it develops, and as Jacques hears the rumors that circulate in the offices of *L'Humanité.*

In addition to the uncertainty of the political developments (for the characters in the novel, and for us as we see from their angle), there is an element of mystery when Jacques, who returns briefly to Geneva, is sent back to Paris and on to Antwerp by Meynestrel, who has him contact a Russian bringing secret documents. In their clandestine meeting, Jacques learns from him about the uprisings in St. Petersburg, at the same time as the Austrian attitude towards Serbia becomes distinctly more aggressive.

When Jacques returns to Paris, he decides to visit Daniel again at the clinic, then suddenly makes an abrupt about-face and goes to find Jenny at the Fontanin home—an act of which he is scarcely aware and whose consequences he certainly does not weigh. He misses her but meets Daniel, who takes him to his studio where he is choosing some paintings to sell before returning to his post. Once again Daniel tries to break down Jacques' resistance and establish a dialogue with him; but Jacques fixes his mind on the political situation and resents his friend's conscious preference of esthetic values and his willingness to turn away from contemporary events.

Since Jenny has seen Jacques, her thoughts return to him constantly, with anger and resentment. The portrait of her is sympathetic; but it also offers an unfavorable contrast with that of Nicole Héquet, who has lost both her children and can never have another. Her griefs, as she presents them to Daniel, are real, whereas Jenny's are founded upon a malaise which, in Marxist terms, is merely the choice of a bored, idle girl of the bourgeoisie. Her mother's obstinate belief that spirit is all (reflected again in these pages during a conversation with Daniel) and her refusal to talk of feelings in ordinary human terms certainly have contributed to Jenny's unhappiness.

On Saturday the 25th Jacques goes to Antoine's house for lunch and meets some of the young men who form his research team. One of these is a faithful reader of the *Action française.*

Martin du Gard's presentation of his points of view, which run counter to the majority of the political views in his writings, shows his ability to comprehend and reproduce a stand not his own—an ability he shared with Gide. Later, Jacques goes to the Gare de l'Est to say goodbye to Daniel. He finds Jenny there too but scarcely addresses a word to her. However, after the train has left, in an inexplicable reversal of behavior in which Martin du Gard skillfully shows the role of chance, he waits for Jenny, confronts her, and insists upon having an explanation with her. When she refuses, he pursues her in a wild chase down the staircases of the subway and through the streets, until at last he forces her to sit in a small square and listen to him—which she does at first unwillingly but then with consent at his voice reveals to her what she had continued to hope: that he loves her. Even then, her consent is grudging, and it is clear that she sees their love as an abyss into which she is letting herself be drawn. Jacques tries to explain his idealism, his abrupt departure four years earlier, his persistent and silent orientation towards her during their absence. They separate with a pledge to see each other the following day.

V *Sunday, July 26-Wednesday, July 29*
(Chapters XXXIX-LIV)

With an increased sense of threat in the atmosphere and a growing precipitation of action, the events of these days center around Jenny and Jacques and his political activities. As though they suspected that little time will be allotted to them, they spend as much of it together as possible and try to make up for all the time they have wasted, to identify their feelings and lives and consolidate their futures. Since Jenny remains reticent and cannot overcome the habit of hiding her feelings to others and living intensely only on the interior plane, most of their commitment is made wordlessly or by understatement. Jacques tries to reveal himself completely, emphasizing his choice of socialism and his devotion to the cause of pacifism and a society freed from capitalism and class divisions. Without any political education whatsoever, Jenny is nevertheless able to follow his exposition and understand his views, for he presents them passionately and yet with concrete facts to support them. Furthermore, she, like Jacques, is an idealist, an absolutist; by

[126]

definition, what is meaningful and true to Jacques will be meaningful to her. Her acceptance, though reticent and underlain by complexes, is total. Their vision of what their own happiness might be—must be—is understood henceforth in terms of a total devotion not only to each other but to the socialist ideal.

Jacques is persuaded both that war may break out at any time—in which he is correct—and that there will be a sufficient pacifist resistance to force the governments to withdraw their threats and make some kind of peace. Thus he is both pessimistic and optimistic. He will retain longer than his associates the belief that united action, or a supreme gesture on the part of a convinced pacifist, can forestall the war. Meanwhile, diplomatic relations are broken between Austria and Serbia. The events are discussed during a Sunday afternoon reception at Antoine's, at which are present not only the two brothers but Antoine's collaborators and his patient, the diplomat Rumelles, who brings him the latest news from the Quai d'Orsay. Rumelles puts up a façade of optimism and justifies with ease, to all except Jacques, the policies of the French government. Later, in a private interview with Antoine, he reveals the underside of the maneuvering at the Quai d'Orsay, the way the government is managing the news, the failure of negotiations and the sure build-up of a mentality of war and revenge—exactly what Jacques has been criticizing.

Jacques receives from Meynestrel instructions to go on a secret mission to Berlin on behalf of the International and to report to him at Brussels on the 29th, during a socialist meeting. It is a question of no less than espionage. Jacques is to transmit to Brussels secret papers stolen from an Austrian officer in Berlin. Again, a detective story element returns, adding tension to an already high-pitched narrative. Jacques is unhappy about leaving Jenny, particularly since her mother has imprudently gone to Vienna to settle matters with Jérôme's creditors. But he places duty to the cause of socialism and pacifism above his personal feelings. In Berlin, he accomplishes his mission without difficulty and also tries to find out how determined the German socialists are to resist the war policies of their government.

Stopping in Brussels, Jacques finds the group from the *Local* and exchanges with everyone points of view on the developing crisis and the proposed action of the European socialist parties.

Views run from his determined optimism to the more realistic recognition that the socialist parties are being gradually forced to accept their government's notion of a defensive war, which they will be morally obliged to support—what will come to be called in France "l'Union sacrée," an alliance of all parties against the invader. Jacques hands over to Meynestrel the documents, which are indeed compromising, for they point clearly to complicity on the part of Austria and Germany (the military establishment of each country, at least) to provoke Serbia and Russia and to force their nations into the war. Such a revelation would mean that the Kaiser and his diplomats could no longer uphold the thesis of a defensive war against encirclement. There might have to be a diplomatic retreat; and in any case, world opinion would be excited against Germany and Austria to the point, perhaps, of damaging their hopes for a profitable and victorious war.

Meynestrel reads the documents alone. The reader has already suspected that there is a serious disparity between the views of the Pilot and other members of his group. He has shown less optimism concerning the prevention of war, has not upheld pacifism, and has concentrated in his remarks on the dialectics of revolution and the probability of a mass uprising in wartime. Here, the omniscient narrator reveals Meynestrel's reasoning, which is that the war must *not* be prevented, since it is the only chance, though not a certain one, of precipitating European revolution at the moment. Because revelation of Austria's and Germany's machinations might slow down the mechanism of threats and alliances leading to the war, Meynestrel decides to burn the papers. Later, he tells Jacques they were of no interest. Jacques will, however, gather evidence enough to make him realize that Meynestrel deliberately destroyed them.

It is a kind of ironic justice—though Jacques does not make the observation—that, the very evening after he has burned the documents which might have led to a clearing of the diplomatic channels and a postponement of the war, Meynestrel should be punished in his personal life. Since the earliest scenes in Geneva where Meynestrel and Alfreda were seen together, along with the English socialist Paterson, Martin du Gard has multiplied the suggestions the Meynestrel was not confident of

Alfreda's devotion and that, perhaps without her realizing it, she leaned more and more on Paterson. Finally the two have realized their mutual love. Pat' announces to Jacques that he is taking Alfreda away to England. Early the next morning Jacques goes to find Meynestrel at his hotel room, just at the moment when he has sorted his papers and moved the furniture in order, presumably, to hang himself. Jacques' arrival puts an end to his project, and he packs his belongings and leaves for Geneva, just as Jacques boards the train to return to Paris.

VI *Thursday, July 30-Saturday, August 1*
(Chapters LV-LXXI)

In the three crowded days between Jacques' return from Brussels and the declaration of general mobilization in France, which is posted on Saturday afternoon, Jacques, Jenny, and Antoine live through a variety of episodes, hopeful and despairing, in a panorama that approaches a cinematographic impression. Martin du Gard switches frequently and abruptly in these pages from one incident to another; from one part of the city to another; from the close-ups of the principal characters to the wide-angled views of crowds milling in the streets; from the personal dramas to the collective drama that is holding an entire continent in suspense. One is reminded of Sartre's similar technique, carried much farther, when he presents in *Le Sursis* the Munich crisis and the barely-averted hostilities of 1938. In both volumes, the oppressive summer heat, frequently mentioned, is used to suggest the atmosphere of danger, of stifling political maneuvering, and of apathy on the part of many whose fate is being decided at the conference tables. Like Sartre, Martin du Gard achieves an impression of near-simultaneity of action, which is suitable at this moment when all Frenchmen are involved in the same drama and personal views are caught up in the civic uncertainty. Moreover, there is an impression of haste—equally suitable to Jacques' desperate efforts to avert the war and to the feelings of patriots like Antoine's collaborator Manuel Roy who is impatient to be enrolled in the Army and devote himself to the cause of *revanche*. This haste is also that of Jacques and Jenny and of the anonymous citizens who are trying to arrange or rearrange their lives before it is too late.

A reflection of this haste is that, throughout these pages, Jacques and Jenny scarcely finish a meal, stay in the same place only briefly, and sleep only fitfully.

Returning to Paris, Jacques learns that more and more supporters of the International are abandoning their policies of struggle against the government to support the nationalist cause in the face of the aggressor. He makes arrangements to liquidate his part of the inheritance from M. Thibault (which he had never wanted to accept but which Antoine had kept for him) in order to give the cash to the Party treasury. Then Jenny accompanies him to a socialist meeting at Montrouge. After a number of speakers have retraced the history of German-French relations since 1870 and given their accounts of the diplomatic maneuvering—suggesting that France must repulse the imminent invasion—Jacques rises to his feet and gives an impassioned speech in defense of pacifism, resistance to conscription, and refusal to support the bourgeois government in any of its imperialistic policies. For him, there is no longer time to discuss theory; he offers a plan of action, which is a general strike and the refusal of all workers to let themselves be drafted.

This same day, Antoine has another discussion with Rumelles, who lets him see the impasse that the government has come to, its impotence to change the system of counter-alliances and alliances, its gradual involvement in the coming war. Russia, all the while talking about arbitration, is mobilizing; when Russia mobilizes, Germany will too, and the war will be a reality. After this conversation, Antoine receives the visit of Simon de Battaincourt, Anne's husband, who asks his advice about his stepdaughter, Huguette, whom Anne has virtually abandoned. Facing for the first time the husband of his mistress, and discovering that he is far from being the egoist that she claims, he suddenly realizes that his liaison is repugnant to him. Without telling Simon of the affair, he decides to break with her, and for several days he refuses to talk with her when she calls or to see her.

A scene which takes place at Antoine's apartment is one of the most revealing of this part. Jacques goes to talk to his brother and finds him involved in a political argument with his collaborators. Antoine finds himself repeating the official optimistic arguments given him by Rumelles. But inside he is tormented, for he realizes that reason is powerless in face of the war hysteria and the gearwork in which Europe is caught. "The storm was shaking the bases on which he had carefully constructed his life: science, reason. He discovered suddenly the impotence of the mind, and before so many unleashed instincts, the uselessness of the virtues on which his industrious life had been founded from the beginning—wisdom, experience, the desire for justice" (II, 516).

After a long passage in which Antoine tries to explain to Jacques the point of view of the English, their reasons for not committing themselves yet, he launches into an argument with Jacques concerning the morality of refusal to be conscripted. Jacques affirms that under no conditions will he allow himself to be made a soldier. Antoine insists that civic duty requires one to accept the view of the majority and to follow the law, whether one approves of it or not. It is the old argument of civil disobedience. Antoine supports the view of the social contract: if one is a member of society, receiving its benefits, one is bound by that contractual agreement to fulfill one's obligations, such as military duty and payment of taxes, without examining the personal convenience or morality of the social standards. Jacques affirms that his first duty is to humanity, not to the specific society in which he has been born, and that there is a moral law higher than any social contract which commands him to respect human life and to refuse to go to war. Such a dispute is insoluble, since the understanding of moral obligation can always vary. The sympathetic portrait Martin du Gard gives of Jacques and his views allows us to realize that the author is sensitive to this moral idealism which is at the basis of conscientious objection. Nevertheless, the arguments put forth by Antoine, though no more eloquent, correspond more closely to the assumptions of much of Martin du Gard's writing—that society is a necessary framework, imperfect but useful, and that individual mysticism leads to anarchy or undermines the habits of duty and solidarity through which most men find their happiness.

After this conversation—into which M. Chasle injects a humorous note, since his trite remarks on the events are most inappropriate to their tragic implication—Jacques and Jenny learn that Germany is mobilizing. The only hope remaining is that a delegate whom the German socialists are sending, Müller, will be able to reach some understanding with the French socialists on methods of resistance, and that the whole proletariat will rise against the governments, thus making war virtually impossible. They go to have late supper in the same cafe with Jaurès. This is the evening of Jaurès' assassination, which occurs before their eyes. It is significant that Martin du Gard chooses to have us witness this event, one of the most important of the pre-war period, through the eyes of a fervent socialist. Jaurès appears to us thus as a great man, the only one capable of holding the line on pacifism, the only one who could unite the workers of Europe in a general strike. Now that he is dead, Jacques feels that there is little practical hope for resistance, and that a great light has gone out from the whole socialist movement. After this disturbing event, and knowing that Jacques' name is probably on the list of suspects, the Carnet B, Jenny invites him to spend the night at the Fontanin apartment.

Saturday, August 1, is the day when the mobilization of France is announced for the 2nd. Jacques feels that the bourgeois governments have succeeded in their aim to provoke the war and increase their prestige and their markets. Jenny dares to ask him what he will do, since he has already made it clear that he will not serve as a soldier. He has no clear plan, though he considers the possibility of returning to Switzerland and working there for the pacifist cause. In a passage clearly foreshadowing the existentialist emphasis on the *act*, Jacques insists that to think, to have convictions, is nothing if one does not carry them out by action (II, 589). He muses on the possibility of finding an act which a single person could carry out and which would hold high the socialist ideal in the midst of the coming war. This is a preparation for his heroic deed at the end of *L'Eté 1914*.

Feeling that it is necessary to tell Antoine of their love and their plans, Jacques and Jenny return to see him. For a moment, there is a sense of fraternity between the two men, stronger even than that which bound them at their father's bedside. A number of Antoine's friends are also present, including his ven-

erated master, Doctor Philip. Philip's views on the inevitability
of events and the "trap of destiny" which history turns out to be
for men may be close to those of Martin du Gard, and in any
case foreshadow the long interrogation that, in the *Epilogue*,
Antoine will make of history and of the possibility of man's
freedom. As they are discussing the war and he expresses his
dismay over what has happened and his conviction that the
European society which he has known will be destroyed forever
by the cataclysm, he makes reminiscences on his life which are
sometimes quoted as being revealing of the way Martin du
Gard saw the principal events of his own life.[4] "I will have had
three somber dates in my existence . . . The first is when the
provincial and pious child that I was discovered, one night,
when reading the four Gospels in a row, that it was a web of
contradictions. The second was when I convinced myself that
a nasty man, named Esterhazy, had done a dirty thing . . . and
that, instead of condemning him, they persisted in torturing in
his stead a man who had done nothing, but who was Jewish . . .
The third is a week ago, when the newspapers published the
text of the ultimatum . . ." (II, 597).

When Jacques takes Antoine aside to tell him of the love
between him and Jenny, the fraternal understanding between
them falls immediately. Both brothers are at fault: Jacques
because he explains too little and expects Antoine to take on
faith, by a sort of intuition, the rarity and the necessity of his
love for Jenny; Antoine because he presents a critical view far
too practical for the situation. His judgment that Jacques is
incapable of making *any* woman happy, under any circumstances, much less now, is probably a fair one. The reader who
has followed Jacques' thoughts and who knows his absolutism
will share this skepticism. Nevertheless, such practical considerations—as Antoine later recognizes when he returns to see
Anne one last time—scarcely apply at moments of crisis. It is
pointless, in any case, for Antoine to try to reason Jacques
out of his love. It is a bitter reflection on human relationships
that at this moment, when events may separate them forever
(they will have only a brief goodbye at the station), they must
leave each other by quarreling, by failing to respect in each
other the individuality which makes them distinct, failing

to realize that life's chief commitments are probably not made on practical grounds but on mystical ones—by that subjective truth of which Kierkegaard spoke. After Jacques leaves, accusing Antoine of never having loved, the latter considers his life, realizes that Jacques is right if love is necessarily this wild romantic passion, and yet has some regret that he has not responded more warmly to Anne's obvious passion; he decides to return to see her once.

The same evening, Jacques and Jenny learn that Müller's visit is without practical consequences, and that Germany has declared war on Russia. In an attempt to bolster his hopes, he repeats the words which Jaurès is supposed to have said at the Brussels meeting: "Maintain the International, no matter what the cost." Their nerves raw, their hopes down, and in a state of extreme fatigue, Jacques and Jenny return to her house and to the bed on which they will sleep together.

VII *Sunday, August 2-Monday, August 10*
(Chapters LXXII-LXXXV)

Like preceding ones, the last chapters of *L'Eté 1914* center on Jacques, his personal life and his political commitment. As the latter becomes more passionate and finally is acted out by a striking gesture, the reader becomes more aware that *L'Eté 1914* is one of the finest presentations of the imperative of political commitment which became central to French fiction in the '30s and '40s, and which remains significant in the literary scene. That the gesture is, empirically, a futile one and that Jacques meets a bitter, meaningless end reveals Martin du Gard's skepticism about the utility of commitment; this does not detract, however, from the powerful portrait of Jacques or from the political consciousness which, however futile, is fundamental throughout the work. The failure of political idealism is one of its chief features in the twentieth century, a lesson as important as that of political involvement. Indeed, as Martin du Gard suggested in *Jean Barois* concerning science and humanistic optimism, there are severe weaknesses in the ideological views inherited from the previous century which have become realities in our time, and a need for constant reevaluation.

It is ironic that Mme de Fontanin, about whom Jenny has worried since her departure for Vienna, should return to Paris the very morning after which Jacques and Jenny have slept together. There is a strained scene during which Jenny drags Jacques into the living room and presents him to her mother as her new authority, her unique love whose destiny is hers. Jenny does not explain sufficiently; she wants her mother to accept by intuition, absolutely (as Jacques had expected with Antoine). It may be supposed that she is fundamentally insecure in this new-found love, to be so hostile about facing it in front of her mother. One sees clearly here what the novelist has subtly suggested before: that Jenny's feelings for her mother are ambiguous.

Martin du Gard qualifies Mme de Fontanin as "pauvre femme" at least three times in this part. Nevertheless (though the portrait is too sympathetic for us to suspect irony), one feels that this needs qualification. Antoine has always found Mme de Fontanin "admirable." But though her nobility of mind may be real, her understanding has severe limits. Jenny's criticism that her mother is egotistical and has wanted to keep her children to herself seems well-founded. The mother treats the idea of Jenny's marriage as preposterous and complains that she was not consulted. Her perpetual reliance upon the "spirit" for counsel and her belief that, having been frank with her children (but she has not been, truly), she has won their confidence forever, are the sort of assumptions which, precisely, raise barriers between generations. She cannot accept the idea that Jenny's destiny is separate from hers, or that her child is a person capable of passions which she has never seen.

In short, Martin du Gard indicates here, as he did throughout *Jean Barois* and *Devenir!* and early parts of *Les Thibault*, that the gulf between fathers and sons, or mothers and daughters, is an inevitable one which, at its best, means difference of view, and at its worst, alienation. Confidence, an illusion, cannot endure any severe crisis. This is merely a counterpart to Jacques' long, unfinished quarrel with his father. Moreover, this unsatisfactory relationship between generations is only one among others: as in Gide's *Counterfeiters*, in a Martin du Gard novel human relationships appear as an endless series of misunderstandings.

Similarly, there has been considerable ambiguity in Jenny's reaction to physical love. Whether one should interpret this as a criticism by the author of the shortcomings of a Puritanical view (which Mme de Fontanin has, in spite of her sensual weakness for Jérôme, and presumably instilled in her daughter) is not certain. When one considers that for Martin du Gard physical relationships, of all kinds, appear as a fundamental fact of human life and carry no stigma, necessarily—though they may be the occasion for deception and suffering—one is tempted to believe that this is a criticism of the Protestant view.[5] In any case, Jenny seems wounded in both flesh and spirit by this night. Her aggressiveness to her mother may be just a cover for the humiliation she feels. Though she consents to Jacques twice that day, it is, without his knowledge, in a spirit of martyrdom which fits well with his own state of mind but which would not augur well for the future.

Jacques, the absolutist, feels himself a dissatisfaction with his new bond, not because it has not brought him joy but because he sees himself, romantically, as having dragged Jenny into an abyss; not the abyss of sexual sin but that of his destiny, with which she is now irreparably identified. His preciously-preserved solitude has, he feels, been attacked, to his own detriment but especially to hers. This feeling is probably shared by most lovers upon realizing the implications of commitments, the uncertainty of the future, the consequences of an affective identification. Jacques feels it more strongly because of his lack of ability to come to terms with the contingencies of life and the weaknesses of his own character. Wanting to view himself tragically, he naturally sees his love as a tragic commitment. And, as is often the case with our insights and prophecies, the future will prove him right simply because he is bent on a destiny which will separate him from Jenny and leave her to her solitude.

Before her intended departure for Geneva with Jacques, Jenny quarrels so bitterly with her mother that she leaves early, not intending to return to her home. Waiting for Jacques in the Gare de Lyon, she nevertheless has a change of heart and decides not to leave now but to wait until a future date when she can take her mother with her to settle in Geneva. When Jacques arrives, she is afraid to tell him of this decision, but of course must announce it. Unwittingly, she brings him a great relief. For he has decided upon a plan of action which must be accomplished without her and which will involve the total sacrifice of himself. When he takes Jenny to a nearby hotel, he knows, then, that this is their last afternoon.

It is the old socialist, Mourlan, who gave Jacques the idea of his act. Despairing of organizing resistance to the war policy in either Germany or France, Mourlan says that the only possibility for interrupting the hostilities is a sudden awakening on the part of the men in the battlefield, an uprising which would spread like a flood. This germinates in Jacques' mind and he conceives the project of flying over the battle lines to distribute leaflets which would bring the pacifist message to the people themselves, the only ones who still have the power to refuse to fight. His departure for Geneva takes on the character of a positive act: it is not sterile protest or a coward's flight from military duty, but the first step in a heroic action.

The very last chapters of *L'Eté 1914* are characterized by their frenzy. Jacques finds Meynestrel in Geneva and tries to persuade him to teach him to fly just enough so that he can get a plane over the front lines. Though it is not immediately apparent, it becomes clear the next day that Jacques' plan is exactly the sort of escape Meynestrel is looking for. His active career is finished, for he cannot recover from Alfreda's betrayal; the most he can do is to make his death a meaningful one. He will fly the plane, and both he and Jacques will face inevitable death after they have distributed the tracts, which will number over a million copies. With this agreement, Jacques leaves for Basle on Tuesday the 4th to complete the arrangements. There are long extracts from the passionate prose which he is going to put into the manifest, in an effort to shock the armies on both sides into lucidity. He appeals to their traditions, their instincts, their working-class solidarity. Above all, he tries to show them that they are being duped into carrying on a war for the middle classes. By the time he completes the document in solitude at Basle, he is feverish and excited to the point of being ill; but, as for Tchen in *Man's Fate,* his sickness means nothing, since he will not live long anyway.

It has been clear from the time when Jacques first conceived his project that it is the expression of a deathwish. This is not to doubt the sincerity of his pacifist convictions and his hope to be of use to mankind. But he chooses this gesture, a supreme one without any possibility of retraction, because he values ultimately only the absolute, not the partial, and because it is a way to possess himself (as Kirilov insists in Dostoyevsky's *The Possessed),* to fulfill his destiny in one great and appropriate act, and to confirm his solitude. The mysticism of self-destruction, by which a man may be useful to the party but above all pursues his own apotheosis, is a familiar one to readers of *Man's Fate.* "No, never before until his arrival at Basle has he, the solitary, felt so definitively alone. And he savors with intoxication the dignity, the power of this total isolation; he no longer wants to leave it, until all is consummated . . . Abruptly, without reason, he thinks: 'I am acting thus only by despair. I act thus only to flee myself. I will not undermine the war. I will not save anyone, anyone but myself. But I will save myself, by accomplishing myself" (II, 706). The moment of lucidity in which he realizes his true motives passes rapidly, but the exaltation remains: he is going to his death, which he chooses. Again, one thinks of writers of a later generation: Malraux, whose characters in *The Conquerors* and *The Royal Way* as well as *Man's Fate* are preoccupied with choosing their own death rather than having it chosen for them; Camus, who spoke of creating for men, by their realization of the absurd, *des morts conscientes.* Death becomes an *act* (II, 715).

Pride and humility are inextricably mixed in Jacques' motivation; wanting himself other, he inevitably wants himself *better;* he also has an ideology behind his mysticism. His visions (for in the train and, later, the morning of the flight, he has both nightmares and real waking visions) contain both a dream of future social equality and a vision of himself accomplished. "A day will come, a day will come! Hearts will beat in unison, equality will come about in dignity and justice. . . . He has arrived at the hour of his life when he can no longer postpone the total gift. Has he ever given himself totally? . . . No, not even, perhaps, to the revolutionary ideal. Not even to Jenny. . . . Only now he knows the gift in which all his being is consumed. The feeling of his sacrifice burns him like a flame. . . . Death consented to is not an abdication: it is the flowering of a destiny!" (II, 708).

His death is, moreover, a protest against the absurd: "his last revolt against the absurdity of the world . . ." (II, 710). It is a refusal of the world, an affirmation of the self. Continuing his analysis of himself which is at the same time mystic and extremely lucid—one of the finest passages of Martin du Gard's psychological analysis—he thinks, "All his acts hold together. . . . His existence has been only a long and spasmodic submission to a mysterious orientation, a fatal chain. And now is the end, the apotheosis. His death shines before him . . . This conscious death is the achievement of his life. It is the condition of this last gesture of fidelity to oneself . . . From his childhood, he has said: no! He has never had any other way of affirming himself" (II, 717). One should note that the author relates this indirectly rather than in the first person in quotation marks, probably to suggest that Jacques' reasoning is pre-verbal, a fundamental feeling which he would not express in the terms the author could choose.

The departures from Basle takes place in the night of August 9-10. The last préparations are recounted briefly. Soon they are in the sky, over the battle zone, ready to throw out the leaflets. Then, inexplicably, the engines stop, the plane starts to fall and it crashes in a crown of fire. When Jacques regains consciousness, he is burnt and wounded, surrounded by French soldiers who wonder whether he is a spy. He cannot reply, for his mouth is injured. Martin du Gard gives through his eyes the sight of the French troops, now in retreat from the front lines, and lets us follow his thoughts as he sees the dead Meynestrel and the wrecked plane, in which all the tracts have burnt without anyone's having read them. The retreat is a débâcle; the impressionistic portrait which the author gives of it is skillful, containing most of the elements of such war novels as Barbusse's *Le Feu*, but with just a few details, and foreshadowing the impressionistic, conscience-directed fresco which

Claude Simon draws of the retreat in 1940 in *La Route des Flandres,* as well as Sartre's *La Mort dans l'âme.*

Jacques is carried by unwilling soldiers back toward a main post. But as the Germans come closer, it becomes more and more risky to take time transporting the awkward stretcher. Meanwhile, the treatment he receives, while not always cruel, is far from kind. The soldiers are rough, without charity, and use obscenities. His mind reflects what is going on until, faint from loss of blood and with too little to drink, he finally passes into undisturbed unconsciousness. From here on, Martin du Gard abandons the limited omniscient viewpoint by which Jacques' consciousness was the center, and returns to authorial omniscience.

Finally the stretcher is taken away to be used for a wounded officer, and Jacques is dumped at the roadside, with only one man responsible for him, and the Germans just a short distance away. The guard, frightened and at a loss to know what to do, shoots him. It is not an easy gesture; to give himself courage, he swears at Jacques' inert body as he shoots, "Fumier!" The comment is a bitter one. Jacques can be seen as a martyr, sacrificed for a people who do not recognize him or understand his charitable intentions. Or he may be seen as a fool, led into the trap of human irony by his own exalted ideas. In any case, the distance between thought and action, between intention and realized deed, between sacrifice and meaningful or useful sacrifice, is underscored by this cruel obscenity.

VIII *Vision in* L'Eté 1914

L'Eté 1914 is both vision and history. It is a superior piece of reconstruction of a crucial moment of the century, in which place is given to the feelings of ordinary individuals as well as to the decisions of diplomats and kings. It is also a vivid eschatological evocation. Idealistic politics appears as a force, less strong in this circumstance than nineteenth century nationalism but capable of transfiguring lives and ultimately perhaps man himself. Jacques' belief, though tempered by his individualism and by a traditional view of human nature, informs not only his own actions but the novel's dominant view of historical events, since they are reflected through his eyes. In a world where traditional sources of value are gone, man appears as the architect of his own fate, and Martin du Gard clearly places in his hands a possibility for progress, and therefore a responsibility. Jacques' unfortunate death is an important qualification to the vision of the book. It suggests that the past, with its modes of thinking and its institutions, is stronger than the vision of the future. Yet, in spite of the cruel irony of his death, Jacques appears as *hero*, and the long passages in which he insists that history is man's possibility (not his fate, as in the strict Marxist view) express a dedication which his sacrifice points up, rather than denying.

It should not be necessary to use comments from outside the book to contend that the socialist vision in *L'Eté 1914* expresses, if not a confident belief of the author's, at least a hope that change in human society is possible. Yet it is worthwhile observing that he wrote to Marcel Arland in 1933, "I hope for a great deal from the lower classes in the cities, the workers. There, in spite of the tares, there are immense possibilities of disinterestedness, of fraternity and spiritual outgoing. If there comes a society where the distribution of goods is less arbitrary and unjust, where every worker has leisure, the luxury of a little joy, the time to think about something other than eating, then . . . we will doubtless see what the ordinary man is capable of doing."[6] Leaving aside the question of organizing a socialist society, the author states at least the view that men have more possibilities than contemporary history and tradition would suggest. It can be proposed that, in having Jacques die, Martin du Gard was killing in himself those impulses toward revolt and lyricism which, he said, inspired the creation of Jacques. But, in the ensuing *Epilogue*, Antoine, the voice of moderation, will regret not having understood Jacques sufficiently, not having allowed him his politics, his idealism—as though giving retrospectively to his vision the value which the circumstances seem to undermine.

CHAPTER 8

Epilogue

I *The Return to the Past*

It is significant that the last part of *Les Thibault* bears the
title of *Epilogue*. Though it has an important structural func-
tion in the whole, it is in a sense a postface, an appended view
after the true ending. Those who would argue that the author
felt closest to Jacques or, at least, preferred him and saw him
as the hero of the novel can support their interpretation by the
fact that, when Jacques dies, *Les Thibault* proper is over.
Antoine's end belongs in the *Epilogue*. This is a valid interpretation. Since Jacques' adolescent venture opens the novel,
it is fitting that in a way his death close it. Certainly, as Antoine
himself feels, a great deal of the spirit of the Thibaults is lost
when Jacques is gone. It would be, nevertheless, unfair to deni-
grate the place of Antoine; and the epilogue is not an accessory
to the novel but *another* ending, the ending which Antoine's
view of the world and his death must give. Moreover, though
the scope of the story narrows since he is the only brother left,
many of his reflections and even his limited acts have to do
with Jacques, retrospectively, and with Jenny and the child she
bore after Jacques' disappearance. The epilogue thus rounds out
not only Antoine's own destiny but also that of the Thibault
family. And, because there is a child, a new generation, it is,
as well as an end, a beginning.

Because the story is centered on one consciousness only, that
of Antoine (though it is told from two points of view, the third
person and then first person), it also furnishes a coherent retrospective view of what has preceded and a sort of judgment by
one of the characters most involved. In this sense, as in others,
it does not belong with preceding volumes but takes its place
apart. There is a commensurate change in tone: what made

the world of the Thibaults for Antoine—his own career, his
father, Jacques and his problems and his idealism, Gise's
freshness, Jenny's youth, the vigor and *joie de vivre* of Daniel—
is all changed, and he surveys himself and his past as one
surveying a disaster, with a sobered view of human projects and a reflective tone, both bitter and resigned. It is appropriate that the chronological moment should be the spring,
summer, and the autumn of 1918—when the four years since
Jacques' death have changed the entire European world, and
civilized man, the armistice notwithstanding, finds blood and
despair much closer than hope. This world is in every way
radically different from the *belle époque* generation of Antoine's
youth, from the comfortable certitudes and the sure successes
of that age. It is itself an epilogue.

Roughly the first two-thirds of the volume are a third-person
narration, with limited omniscience as the technique, to tie up
the loose narrative ends. After a first wound in the chest, from
which he recovered easily to return to the front, Antoine was
gassed in November, 1917, and since then has been treated in
two different clinics. When the volume opens, he is in the south
and is undergoing detoxification treatment. His interests center
on his own convalescence, of which he does not question the
ultimate success, and on the war, with which he is obsessed,
without either approving wholeheartedly the Allied position or
wishing, as Jacques had, to devote himself to an anti-war cause.
He is disabused: doubting certain victory, doubting the success
of post-armistice peace construction, not believing in the nationalist propaganda but realizing that the war must be fought
anyway. Many of his reflections on the war, on political theory
and reality, and on the nature of man and man's destiny may be
taken as expressions of the author's own opinion. Perhaps
more than anywhere else, Martin du Gard is speaking here
through a *porte-parole*.

Antoine receives a telegram telling of Mademoiselle de Waize's
death and decides to go to Paris for the funeral and to take advantage of the occasion to consult with Dr. Philip. During the
chapters which take place in Paris and at Maisons-Lafitte much
of the background is filled in. One of the first subjects of this
gradual exposition is Jacques. His death was verified only

after several months of investigations, thanks in part to Antoine's friend Rumelles. It is decided that he was burned in the plane which went down. No one suspects the real end of Jacques, although, by intuition, Jenny senses that the official version of his death is not quite accurate. When Jenny was expecting her child, she went to Switzerland to have it and to meet those who had known Jacques. From that time forward she has devoted herself to the memory—the cult—of Jacques and to raising her child, whose illegitimacy she accepts as a token of his father's free thought.

Gise, Abbé Vécard, and M. Chasle are the only familiar faces at Mlle de Waize's funeral. It is when Gise sees Antoine and is taken aback by his thinness and his horrible cough that the novelist suggests for the first time that Antoine's convalescence may not be as rapid as he hopes, or as certain. Gise and Antoine return to the Thibault house, normally deserted. It is a painful kind of sentimental journey, in which Antoine meets not only the shadows of the dead and those who have irrevocably changed, but his own image as he was in the prime of his career, when he set up the elaborate laboratories. Ghosts of the past wait for him at every corner, his office, Jacques' room, the buffet where Mademoiselle stored her pomades. Gise tells him in detail about the military hospital which Mme de Fontanin started at Maisons-Lafitte, using the Thibault villa which Antoine had opened to her, in which Jenny, Nicole Héquet, and Gise all work as nurses. She persuades Antoine to visit Maisons-Lafitte.

Before going there, however, he has dinner with Rumelles at Maxim's, in a scene worthy of Proust. In his particular jargon, but very freely, Rumelles airs to Antoine his views of the European war, the current French government, the attitude of Wilson and the offers of the Americans, and the practice of politics in general. He is more disabused than Antoine, for he has built his whole life around diplomacy and yet feels that in the long run no man is master of his political fate, no diplomat can do much more than disguise events momentarily, give them a name and a language, and act as a shield between political realities and the desires of the country. He manages the news; he does not make it. Along with this disillusionment, there is the cynicism of a fatigued man, one who has seen the war from offices and has little notion of the physical conditions indicated by the news dispatches. Antoine, though not excessively idealistic, finds Rumelles superficial and petty in his criticisms of the Americans, offhanded in his discussion of the war.

Antoine's visit to Maisons-Lafitte is, also, a pilgrimage back to the past, with a certain feeling of nostalgia: he had spent his summers at the villa, and he imagines Jacques there as though time had turned. From both Jenny and Gise he learns of the strange friendship which has united them since Jacques' death. Sharing a love for the same man—a love which will not die and will know no replacement—and feeling that they alone appreciated Jacques, they are drawn together. Yet, essentially, each one is still alone in her individual love for the dead man's memory, and there reigns between them, as well as affection, an obvious jealousy. Antoine also learns how Mme de Fontanin's character has developed, yet remained identical, since she began doing useful work for the wounded. On the one hand, her patriotism has made her accept wholeheartedly the official nationalist propaganda. She has given of herself without reserve and recognizes, wisely, that a life of idleness would no longer suit her. In a way, she does not want the war to end. On the other hand, she has maintained her stubborn belief, second only to that of Pastor Gregory, in the victory of spirit, the non-existence of evil, and the involvement of a personal God in her own life, as indicated by her extrasensory perception.

More enigmatic is the case of Daniel. Since his wound and amputation in the war, he has been at the hospital, living on his pension, offering no help, and not even pursuing his painting, which, with his love affairs, had been all his life. He is changed apparently even in temperament: no longer vivacious, he is phlegmatic, docile, and plays nursemaid for the little Jean-Paul. Antoine does not cease to wonder at the transformation, which is too great to be explained only by an artificial leg. It is only later, through a letter to Antoine, that Daniel reveals what has changed him and what, he believes, will lead ultimately to his suicide: the loss of his sexuality in the explosion. The theme of sterility, which has already appeared, is carried out with Daniel, as it is with Gise, whose entire life is going to be devoted to raising the child of another woman and perpetuating the memory of a dead love which was not even requited. There is, in Gise as well as Jenny, a Jamesian quality which may be characterized as the attitude of unreconciled resignation.

Upon returning from Maisons-Lafitte, Antoine pays to his professor Dr. Philip a visit which turns out to be crucial, and which will cause a rupture in the narrative line. Though Philip tries to be optimistic about Antoine's injury, he is in reality very much concerned and he subjects Antoine to an examination. The passage is narrated primarily from Antoine's point of view; but Martin du Gard gives sufficient indications, through Philip's gestures and comments, that the latter is struck by Antoine's terrible condition and that he does not want to let his former pupil see how much he is worried. He keeps up his chatter about the war—expressing his skepticism concerning the possibilities of the European powers to organize a democratic society after the near-dictatorship of the war governments. As Antoine is preparing to leave, he turns around suddenly to catch Philip in an unguarded moment and sees written clearly on his face the verdict which he had tried to hide: Antoine is doomed. The judgment is mute but clear. He leaves in a state of despair unlike anything he had ever experienced.

He starts wandering through the streets, just as an air raid comes. The Parisian landscape under the sirens, with shadows and muffled voices, is masterfully evoked; it recalls the poetical air raid scenes in *Le Temps retrouvé*. Antoine's solitude is juxtaposed to the horror and beauty of the city under the raids—the Concorde in its eery light, the fleeing shapes, the estrangement of the buildings and their inhabitants. Antoine is estranged from himself as he is seized with the consciousness of himself as a mortal creature whose death is imminent. Death is in the sky, in the streets; death is in him. He recognizes his ultimate, irrevocable solitude—the solitude which is man's lot always (as the existentialists have insisted)—against the solitude of a deserted city and a threatened civilization.

II *Antoine's Diary*

The remainder of the *Epilogue* consists of a few letters and of Antoine's journal, kept during the four and a half months before his death. Martin du Gard said that the composition of this journal was easy and rapid for him—a feat when one considers that the author was at the time neither so young as his hero nor so sick (I, cxvi). The capacities of his imagination (often overlooked as he is praised for his powers of observation) are proved in the passages where he writes, in the first person, of a sure, imminent death, of the horrors of progressive physical ruin, of the disappointment of a man whose career lay before him like a promise. For years, Antoine had lived on the future— "after the war." Deprived of this future, he sees that he has done little and has not exhausted, as Valéry reminds us to do, the "field of the possible." He realizes in a Meursault-like intuition that life consists of the present, and that the arbitary end of life which fate assigns to us places retrospectively on our experience the high price of the irreplaceable.

The letters bear some essential information which leads into Antoine's journal. First, we learn by a note from Daniel of his impotence. The revelation is heightened by being made at the time when Antoine learns of his own incurable illness and starts to become very much preoccupied with Jenny's son Jean-Paul. Moreover, he receives a letter from a nurse who had cared for Rachel in her last days as she died of yellow fever. This brings even more to Antoine's attention the absurdity of death, against the background of the absurdity of life. All Rachel's passion ended in a sordid hospital room in the tropics, where, as he will, she died alone.

The diary has a straight chronological structure but a rather rich thematic one. The chronological line is double: the gradual weakening of Antoine's lungs, heart, and energies; and the progress of the allied armies throughout August, with the speeches of Wilson and the growing possibility of the end of the war. That Antoine's end should come as the armistice is being signed (he dies on November 18) is a clear irony. He takes a considerable interest in the advance of the Allies and the efforts of peacemakers, including Wilson, to construct the peace as a new order, rather than a simple reshuffling of boundaries and colonial possessions. Yet he is appalled in a way by his own interest, as he realizes that he will not be there to witness the rebuilding of Europe.

Since the diary form is free, the author takes advantage of it to move rapidly among a variety of topics that preoccupy Antoine and which, one may surmise, were equally important for him: the war, of course, and death; the chances for peace and a democratic society; the solutions which religion proposes to a dying man and, more generally, for all the daily questions of human belief and behavior; the general problem of human motivation and ethics; the role of medicine (here Martin du Gard's analyses are clinical—too much so, for the abundant medical terms do not make any more real for the average reader the sense of death or the concrete effects of illness, whereas they cloud the more generalized statements about approaching death). Antoine muses additionally upon heredity and his only heir, Jean-Paul, the one with the blood of the Thibaults and the Fontanins; on love, which he fears he has not sufficiently known; and, more generally, upon the possibilities of human progress and the meaning of an individual destiny.

It would be tedious to follow in detail his reflections. They can be divided into two groups: those which tend toward an acceptance of his lot and a total view of human evolution in which his own place is small, but real; and those which are closer to despair, in which he regrets bitterly the loss of his youth and his energy but particularly of his future, and finds that whatever the destiny of the race, an individual can find no reconciliation with his own death. Death is the end of *his* possibilities. Less than bitterness, Antoine feels a terrible discouragement at contemplating his annihilation. At moments when he nonetheless achieves a certain perspective and tranquility, he finds consolation in two prospects; the future of Jean-Paul and the possible (though not certain) amelioration of the human fate, particularly of the European politicial situation.

Jean-Paul, who has in his veins the energy of the Thibaults, the stubbornness of his grandfather, the practicality of his uncle, and the idealism of his father may realize all the possibilities which the previous generation could not bring to fruition. Antoine addresses Jean-Paul personally in parts of his diary and intends to leave for him some of his personal and medical papers. Unfortunately, even this hope, which is the most concrete he will allow himself, is ultimately seen as ironical, since, when he speaks of "you, Jean-Paul, in 1940," the reader cannot fail to consider the tragic repetition of history and the end of hope for so many young Frenchmen in 1940.

As for the future of the race, Antoine thinks that there may be improvement if the fresh idealism of the Americans can correct the closed imperialism and petty politics of the European powers. He places some hope in the idea of the League of Nations. Looking farther ahead, he supposes that history is moving gradually towards improvement of the human species, a better organization of his society, and the creation of a human ethics more successful than either religious ethics or nineteenth century humanistic morality. This is one of the legacies of the previous century to Martin du Gard: his rooted belief, in spite of his pessimistic view of contemporary history, that man is a creature evolving towards a better organization, and that the meaning of life, insofar as one can speak of it, is this slow, ultimately successful movement towards the perfection of the species.

Antoine refuses the consolation of religion. In a scene which resembles the visit of the chaplain to Meursault in *The Stranger* and which must have excited Camus' admiration, the hospital priest tries to persuade Antoine to accept the sacraments and not to "die like a dog." Since he does not believe, this hypocrisy would be intolerable to him. Trying to decide what may be values and standards for living, he realizes that he has practiced (though perhaps not with the spontaneity or thoroughness he should have) an ethics of individual choice. Like Bernard and others in *The Counterfeiters* and so many existentialist heroes of the next generation, he decides that *he* must choose, irrespective of others' choices, and then pursue his values steadfastly. Only then can one be *authentic*. Since there are no absolute values and no standards suitable for all, authenticity, or fidelity to one's own requirements and beliefs, becomes the supreme value which could be, in an individual way, shared by all men. One notes again the Sartrian overtones (II, 948). This, and the practice of a responsible skepticism, seem to him the best ethical standards to write down for Jean-Paul.

In the end, his diary is a mixture of optimism and pessimism, of understanding and despair. Like Camus, he says that he has "lived in optimism" (II, 965). Yet he realizes that life is a derision, not only for him, dying in the prime of his years through two stupid war accidents, but for all the young men he saw agonizing who, like him, will not see the morning of a new Europe. As a scientist, with a perspective on the world of the infinitely small as well as the world of space and time (he meditates at night, looking at the stars), he sees that man is a small thing, an accident in a world of natural accidents, without inherent meaning and in whom it is useless, nay wrong, to seek for meaning. This perspective can bring a certain calm. For all his understanding, however, as he looks back over his own life he admits, simply, "I am condemned to die without having understood much about myself, nor the world" (II, 964).

From the diary, we learn that Antoine has wanted to marry Jenny, in a purely formal arrangement, so that her son will have the name Thibault legally. With her usual pride and obstinacy, she refuses, speaking of the glory of freeing oneself from bourgeois prejudice. Antoine regrets her decision but resigns himself to it. We also witness his ambiguous feeling about other men—with whom he feels a strange fraternity since his condemnation, from whom, nevertheless, he is separated. It is Camus' paradox of "solidarity, solitude," to which all men are susceptible. Antoine also alludes in his diary to his decision to take his own life once he comes so close to death that the agony is unbearable and the mastery of his own destiny is nearly gone. In the last pages this decision becomes an obsession. When he is operated on for an abscess, he wonders why he has not already taken the fatal dose. As the armistice is signed, he is so weak that he is incapable of following the events and continuing his diary. On the 18th of November, he adds his last lines to the page: "Simpler than you think. Jean-Paul." Again using the privilege of choosing euthanasia, he has at least possessed his own death, in a different way from his brother but with the same stoical determination.

III   *Time and Possibility*

T. S. Eliot's lines from "Burnt Norton" could serve as an epigraph for Antoine's journal:

> Time present and time past
> Are both perhaps present in time future,
> And time future contained in time past.

Epilogue

. . . .

> What might have been is an abstraction
> Remaining a perpetual possibility
> Only in a world of speculation.[1]

For his obsessive meditations center around the question of time as possibility: time lost for him, for Jacques, for M. Thibault; future time for Jean-Paul, the two somehow connected. Proust's esthetic solution to the problem of lost time is foreign to his temperament, as is any mystic or religious consolation. Antoine has found his self-identity in his activity as a doctor, and this identification becomes impossible as death approaches. He then identifies himself with his thought, but of course this too will be extinguished. So he tries to identify with a historic or cosmic purpose in which time past can be redeemed. "Only through time time is conquered," wrote Eliot. Antoine's life, which is a victim of time (he counts the days, watches the season change), looks forward to the time that still belongs to Jenny, to Jean-Paul, to a whole generation. Though the scope of the *Epilogue* is less vast than that of previous parts, and though it is subject to some criticism, it has a poignancy which reflects back over the whole of *Les Thibault* and gives to the reader that sense of a whole, if tragic, destiny in time which makes a novel memorable.

In *Les Thibault* the circular movement that characterized *Jean Barois* is replaced by a subtler two-directional structure in which both Jacques and Antoine move along separate lines to different ends which are not the same as their point of departure. Although the ends are in each case a betrayal of their hopes, there is a greater sense of freedom within the novel because of the continual contrast between the two brothers and the sense of choice. One might be tempted to conclude that multiplying the points of view and the trajectories within the novel points to a kind of human liberty. Certainly the *Epilogue* indicates, in spite of moral and physiological sterility and the uselessness of the deaths, an open direction in which history may move.

CHAPTER 9

Naturalism Revived: Short Fiction and Plays

I Vieille France

THE myth of the innocence of country life and the nobility of soul of the *petit peuple de France* has rarely been more thoroughly undermined in a literary work than in the naturalistic novel *Vieille France*.[1] Written in 1932, while Martin du Gard had ceased composition on *Les Thibault*, it is the underside of the bourgeois and intellectual society he was depicting in his long novel, and of the humanistic idealism which both Antoine and Jacques lived by. It belongs to a centuries-old literary tradition: just as the idealization of pastoral life is found in virtually all periods of French literature, particularly in the Romantic movement, the realistic view of the peasant occurs in the medieval *fabliaux*, the scathing portrait by La Bruyère, and among the realistic novelists of the nineteenth century who reacted against the Romantic idealization. Unlike contemporary novelists who have portrayed the lives of the lower classes, whether villagers or city workers, with a clear aim of awakening the social conscience of the readers and perhaps defending a particular political view, Martin du Gard seems closest, in his scenes of rural and village life, to Balzac, Flaubert, Zola, and Maupassant whose aim was accuracy, not social revolution.

In a letter to Jean Schlumberger, the novelist qualified *Vieille France* as a collection filled with ugly faces and greedy hearts.[2] The term "album of sketches" which he uses in the dedication is appropriate, for the book is not a novel presenting evolution of characters, but rather a series of scenes concerning the villagers in the small burg of Maupeyrou. The place furnishes unity to the sketches; but a more fundamental unity comes from the outlook, common to nearly every character, and from the novelist's tone—sarcastic and bitterly satirical. Moreover, Martin du Gard has arranged the portraits around a few simple intrigues, all of which take place in one day. This unity of time, scene, and tone gives the book coherence and force which it would not have otherwise.

Only two or three short passages in the book present an explicit authorial judgment; elsewhere, the conclusions are suggested by the conversations and thoughts of the characters themselves and by an artful juxtaposition of details. The first character who appears is the postman, who circulates through the village and the various scenes, giving his own unity to the book. He appears as a rapacious, lecherous, and malevolent mischief-maker, who reads others' letters, writes anonymous notes of accusation, manipulates friends and enemies alike, and controls the village like an evil spirit. Except for the success of his manipulations, his character is not exceptional in the village. From the clerical party through the pensioned war veterans, everyone (save a senile old hermit) thinks only of exploiting others for his advantage. Sexual mores are those of the worst sensationalist literature. Nowhere, however, does the novelist indulge in lurid scenes: the adulteries, incests, and prostitutions are presented by sardonic allusions, with the innuendos which are probably those used by such people themselves in speaking of the scabrous.

In his rounds, the postman visits almost everyone whom he can either use for his ends or persecute gratuitously. Only a few figures seem less avaricious than he: an old lady who is looking for a family with whom to take room and board, in exchange for payment; the priest, who is cowardly and ineffectual but not corrupted inside; the senile recluse, who in his endless babbling to himself retains a pathetic idealism and dreams about a society where money will disappear and all will live under the protection of the state; and the schoolteachers, brother and sister. The priest verbalizes his criticism as he gardens and in his prayers, in which he asks God's forgiveness because he cannot love these terrible people. The schoolteachers are socialists and dream of the revolution. But the man's idealism is sorely cut into by his own marriage, with dirty wife and children and insufficient money or even time to think; and the spinster sister, though trying to keep the socialist faith, has moments of despair and even dreams that her brother assassinates his wife.

These enclaves of reflection and social conscience are swallowed in the village society as a whole, with its superstition and greediness and bestiality. The end of nearly every chapter is an additional insinuation of moral misery. The question that the schoolmistress asks, "Is it the fault of society? . . . Couldn't it be the fault of Man?" (II, 1102) is, in its blunt form, the same question Antoine pours over in his diary, after having discussed it with Jacques: is there not something in man's character which makes him, in spite of social organization, turn on others, go to war, destroy his own aspirations? In an exchange with Marcel Arland concerning *Vieille France,* the author assured him that what he felt when looking at these people was not hate but rather desperation.[3]

Insofar as the author provides insight into the reasons for the ugliness and greediness of the villagers, he attributes this to centuries of struggling for a living, toiling against the soil and against human competition. One notes again the importance he gives to background and heredity. To an extent, then, the economic system seems to blame (and the American reader is likely to agree with this). But, as the priest observed, the medieval French peasant, though perhaps rapacious, had not deserted God. Economics does not seem to be all, and one returns to the schoolmistress's question.

II   Confidence africaine

In a very different vein from *Vieille France,* the story *Confidence africaine* (1931) is nevertheless in the naturalistic tradition by its subject matter. It is exceptional in Martin du Gard's work by being told in the first person. Moreover, there are two narrators: Martin du Gard himself, who addresses a letter to a friend, editor of a review, who had asked him for a contribution; and within this text, the "confidences" of the chief character, who told them to Martin du Gard during a boat trip and which the novelist wrote down. The traditional device of the true story told to the novelist by the character is used here probably not as a mere technical presentation but in order to suggest, not the verisimilitude but the factual truth of the story. For it is the revelation of an incestuous love between a brother and a sister. That the narrative strikes one as being true—although the author said it was an invention—is indicated by the fact that some readers refused to believe he had written the story entirely from his imagination (I, cxxvii).

Neither the author as narrator nor the character as narrator exploits the subject in a lurid manner. Leandro confides in Martin du Gard chiefly to help him see that life *does* contain the extraordinary events which critics accuse novelists of creating against all probability. Martin du Gard sends the narrative to his friend as it is, with simple language and neither justification nor blame. He is suggesting that this is the way life is, and drawing no conclusions.

Martin du Gard first meets Leandro at the sanatorium where he is staying with his supposed nephew, who is dying. After the burial, and after a long visit to the North African city where Leandro lives—during which Martin du Gard meets all his family—the two return to France by boat, and Leandro explains that his nephew was really his son. Raised without a mother, by a tyrannical old father, he and his sister discovered in their teens their mutual attraction and had a passionate love affair for four years. His sister wanted to conceive a child before Leandro had to leave for his military duty, and before her father forced her to marry a middle-aged man with money. When Leandro returned from the army, he discovered his sister settled in conjugal routine, with other children and with no interest in him. The affair was forgotten, and the three of them lived together among the numerous children. The child of incest was congenitally weak; though Leandro loved him, he recognized that his death was a relief for everyone.

The subject matter of *Confidence africaine* recalls the episodes of *Les Thibault* concerning Hirsch, Rachel, and Anne in which abnormal sexual tastes are clearly indicated, and the suggestion of incestuous passion between Jacques and Gise, particularly in "La Sorellina." The tone here is flatter: the extraordinary is deflated and made to seem ordinary. The results of the incestuous love—with the exception of the son's weakness and death—are not unusual. Our interest is psychological, not prurient, and if anything, the episode would indicate that sexual perversions, like all sexual love, succumb to the dullness of time and the erosion of contours that comes with changing circumstances. In *Confidence africaine* as well as *Les Thibault* and *Un Taciturne,* the author looks at sexuality much as Antoine looks at the microbes in his laboratory—a curious facet of natural life.[4]

III   Le Testament du Père Leleu

Paul Léautaud has claimed that the peasant farce, *Le Testament du Père Leleu,* is perhaps the best work of Martin du Gard.[5] It requires a most particular view of literature to prefer the author's plays to his novels, and *Le Père Leleu* (played first in 1914), though showing a fine sense of theater and language, should not be put in the same superior category as his short fiction or *Les Thibault.* As Gaëtan Picon has observed, Martin du Gard's dramatic works are "savory, but without much scope *[portée]*".[6] Like *Vieille France,* they are without profound ties to the vision in the fictional works. They do, however, increase our understanding of the range of the author's view, as they add to his work a comic note which elsewhere is not common.

Le Père Leleu, like the following play, *La Gonfle,* is written in authentic Berrichon dialect. The language itself is a source of much of the humor, as in *The Tales of Br'er Rabbit.* Much of this is lost to the American reader; furthermore, on the stage it must be more striking than in the text. Another source of humor, earthy but not bitter, is the portrait of peasant manners. The avarice, cleverness, and crudity of the peasants appear through a classic situation revolving around money, death, and relations between men and women—the areas in which, as in *Vieille France,* the lower classes show most frankly their reactions and their values.

The three-act drama is simple: the servant, La Torine, who has been hoping to inherit her master's property at his death, is in a rage when he dies before making his testament. She persuades a neighbor, Père Leleu, to dress up like the dead man and dictate his will to the notary before the death is announced.

Cleverer than she, he tells the notary that he will leave all his goods to his good neighbor Leleu. Recalling *La Farce de Maître Pathelin*, it is the plot of the tables turned and returned, of the cheater cheated. Character portraits are excellent; each personage reveals himself only partly to his fellows but wholly to the audience through his asides and his manipulations. Traditional jokes about death and cuckoldry recur, in a tone of farce and good humor, unlike the sardonic humor of *Vieille France*.

IV   La Gonfle *(1922-24)*

Likewise in three acts but longer, *La Gonfle* (which has not been produced, to my knowledge) is similarly a war of peasant wits and a case of the duper duped. Its plot is considerably more complicated than that of *Le Père Leleu*, and its range of humor much cruder. Physical functions, and in particular the circumstances of a pregnant mute servant girl, are the chief subject for humor. In addition to the plots revolving around this pregnancy and the severe dropsy of the mistress, La Bique, a great deal of earthy humor is introduced by an amazing character, Andoche, the sacristan and the consort of La Bique. He is surely one of Martin du Gard's most vivid character creations. Like the postman in *Vieille France*, he is a manipulator, less gratuitously so and more subtly, since he dupes the veterinarian and his own mistress simply by means of language—by suggesting to them what he would have them do.

As he watches the veterinarian solve the problem of the servant's child and the mistress's dropsy, and unwittingly arrange matters to Andoche's liking, he carries on an unending monologue of jokes revolving around priests, pregnancies, and inheritances, seasoned with observations on life and ample vulgarities. His invention (for the stories are mostly made up on the spot) is rich in colorful language and metaphors, and the practical wisdom which comes out, while not lofty, is keen and workable. While language is not rearranged in *La Gonfle*, the creative use to which it is put and the wealth of jokes, forming a total vision of life, as well as the earthiness of the humor, make the English reader think of James Joyce. Moreover, though the plot is well carried out and there are lively scenes of character confrontation, Andoche's monologue is such an essential part of the text that, leaving aside practical reasons for not presenting the play, the work seems less dramatic than fictional.

V Un Taciturne

With the portrait of a successful businessman who discovers in his middle age a hopeless homosexual love for his secretary, Martin du Gard, in *Un Taciturne* (1931), leaves the world of peasant humor and *moeurs de campagne* to return to the portrait of character. Unlike a number of his contemporaries, he did not make of homosexuality an important topic in his work. Yet it is clear that sexual aberrations, just like normal sexual passion, attracted his observer's and psychologist's eye. Between Anne de Battaincourt and her daughter's governess there was a suggestion of abnormal interest. In *Un Taciturne,* in addition to Thierry's passion there is a corresponding Lesbian passion between his sister and an old schoolfriend. Thus, although the tone and the language of *Un Taciturne* are far removed from the earthiness and the farcical or bitter humour of *Vieille France* and the peasant farces, by its subject matter the play revives the genre of realistic and naturalistic psychological drama of the end of the nineteenth century.

Martin du Gard had admired as a youth the creations of Antoine in the theater and the dramatic works of Henri Bernstein, Henry Bataille, Georges de Porto-Riche, and others who specialized in somber psychological and family dramas. His own scenic gifts and his interest in the hidden dramas in men's lives had inspired him to create much of *Jean Barois* and *Les Thibault* around crucial encounters within a family and the passions that drive men, under the surface of their daily occupations. Writing *Un Taciturne* allowed him to consider some of these passions which did not fit into the scheme of *Les Thibault* and to express in particular his views of the sexual problem.

The play is well constructed, in three acts with a change of scene and some intervening time; the characters are drawn carefully. But in a decade when Giraudoux and Cocteau were writing their more imaginative plays, and Antoine Artaud's "theater of cruelty" and other experimental ideas were current, Martin du Gard's psychological study did not have, in spite of its qualities, the originality to attract wide public attention, and it remains more dated than *Les Thibault*.

Thierry and Isabelle are the son and daughter of a businessman who mysteriously committed suicide at an advanced age. Isabelle's past is darkened by years spent in a reform school after she tried to stab Wanda, a fellow schoolgirl, in a fit of jealousy with Lesbian overtones. Thierry has taken care of Isabelle since then, and she devotes herself to him in a relationship which is more like that of old lovers than of siblings. A disabused cousin, Armand (whose matter-of-fact comments on love, life, and death form a sort of chorus in the play and make him probably a spokesman for the author), has loved Isabelle hopelessly for years. Wanda too is now associated with the business, and she and Isabelle affect a warm friendship which is really poisoned by Wanda's passion for her. In this family affair where no relationship could be qualified as normal arrives an ambitious young man, Joë, who persuades Thierry to hire him as a secretary. He courts Isabelle, at first in vain, for she insists that she should not marry with her unfortunate past (only one of the allusions to heredity). Wanda and Armand both observe this courtship and suffer from it, in silence.

When Isabelle reveals to Thierry that she has accepted Joë's love and is engaged to him, Thierry flies into a rage and determines to ruin their plans, to save Joë, he says, from the debilitating tie of marriage. It takes Wanda's own jealousy and Armand's lucid understanding to make Thierry realize that it is because he loves Joë passionately that he cannot accept the idea of his marriage. Thierry has displayed throughout a hearty disapproval of sexual aberrations and has insisted on perfection in all matters. Armand, who considers that such accidents are a part of human nature, assures him that it can happen in the best of families—just as Thierry's father had, it seems, killed himself for love of a girl in her teens. Thierry's intransigence will not allow him to adopt this amoralistic view. Or perhaps it is despair of ever having Joë's love: whatever the reason, he shoots himself. Again, human activities have been at crosspurposes, with everyone except the young couple loving the wrong person; and the image of human relationships is somber indeed. The family seethes with misunderstandings and impasses. Only

Joë and Isabelle can expect some kind of future; and, given the element of heredity, the play would suggest that even they are likely to discover estrangement. *Un Taciturne* has the same charged atmosphere, sense of fatality, and misunderstandings as a François Mauriac novel, without the possibility of redemption one finds in *Viper's Tangle*, without the lucidity and human idealism which, in *Les Thibault*, offer some possibility for self-fulfillment.

CHAPTER 10

Values and the Novel

IN his Nobel Prize speech in Stockholm on December 10, 1937,
Martin du Gard stated what he considered to be the *raison
d'être* of the contemporary novel:

> It was still young when I discovered, in a novel by Thomas Hardy,
> this reflection in one of his characters: *The real value of life seemed
> to him to be less in its beauty than in its tragedy.* That corresponded
> to a profound intuition in me, closely tied to my literary vocation.
> From that time on, I thought (I still think) that the principal object
> of the novel is to express the tragic quality of life. I will add today:
> the tragic quality of an individual life, the tragedy of a destiny
> *being accomplished.*[1]

This understanding, closer to Malraux's excellent formula that
the novel is "a privileged means of expression of human tragedy,"[2] than to realistic traditions of the nineteenth-century novel,
supports Martin du Gard's claim to be our contemporary. That
the novelist's point of departure was the realistic novel of
Tolstoy and that his philosophical view resembles that late
nineteenth century pessimism of which Hardy was the most
outstanding example only add to his achievement of adapting
an inherited form to contemporary preoccupations. The trajectory of an individual life becomes, in Martin du Gard's major
novels, not a case history but an illumination of the tragic
quality of all life, against a background of philosophical questioning and political unrest which is the collective tragedy
of our times.

Those readers who are interested in formal experiments or
those, like Nathalie Sarraute, for whom the nineteenth century
novel is an inaccurate, unauthentic form because of its presup-
positions, would insist that the modern consciousness of the
tragic quality of life should be seized, and molded, in a new

form. It is part of André Malraux's achievement that he did this. Martin du Gard's more classical understanding of literary form is not, however, to be scorned. Like his admired predecessors in the novel, he believed that, as Henry James put it, any form which makes the most of its subject is the correct form—any form by which the novelist can express his vision; and he did not reject those nineteenth century narrative prerogatives of omniscience, authorial exposition, and authorial judgment which could help him draw his subject out of the shadows. If we may grant any fictional conventions, even the minimum one of verbalizing and writing on paper, we may certainly grant those others which an author uses to good effect. Changes in points of view, breaks in narrative time, intrusions into characters' minds, and summarizing judgments do not detract from *Les Thibault,* but rather allow the novelist to handle a wide scope of physical action and psychological study which he could not manage with only one of the more rigorous, but more restricted, devices such as scenic presentation, strict point of view, the diary form, and the like.

That Martin du Gard should make this choice to subordinate the pursuit of beauty or rigor of technique to the needs of a subject indicates that his esthetic is essentially utilitarian and that in literature he gives the primary role to discursive expression of insights or characters who have their own value. Though protesting against the polemical literature of the middle decades of the century, he was not adverse to a literature of *ideas,* with a content. His writings are dramatic, historical, and psychological but not poetical. A passage from his Journal expresses his own awareness of this esthetic: "Always the eternal question of form and content. Haedens considers it absurd for one to separate them. And I insist that one can; that I do so; and you wouldn't have to push me hard to make me declare that one should do so. . . . To me, form and content are as distinct as the rabbit and the sauce" (I, cviii). If, in a generation of experimentation in literary forms and a pursuit of pure form in the novel as in painting, this view of the novel as a container seems pedestrian, it is more than likely that readers in future generations will return to *Jean Barois* and *Les Thibault* and, tolerating the forms which may no longer be current, read them for their content: the portrait of manners, the psychological analyses, and the historical frescoes.

It remains true, nevertheless, that it is for style that we return to many writers whose perceptions seem unimaginative and that, among the greatest French writers, style and content both draw us back (one thinks, in their different genres, of Racine and Pascal, of Stendhal and Proust). What value one may give to Martin du Gard's fictional style—insofar as it can be separated from the content—is a moot point. He is often accused of flatness—a flatness achieved, perhaps, deliberately in the interests of exactness, but perhaps stultifying. Marcel de Coppet wrote to him in 1920:

This turn of mind, this tone, this specific flavor, this particularity of thought and expression, this quality that you alone possess, I see it constantly in your conversation, in your correspondence; but never in your works. As soon as you take up your novelist's pen, it seems that the effort of creation, the technical skill, an excessive concern for correct and proper style, smother your original gifts and make what you write banal (I, lxxxiv).

Shortly thereafter, both Gaston Gallimard and Gide told him that he should work less on his style. "It is," said Gallimard, "by naturalness, simplicity, and spontaneity that you will give to your novels their perfect form. Let others pursue . . . a bold syntax, the rare epithet. . . . Be happy with a clear, correct, unadorned style . . ." (I, lxxxv).

One not familiar with Martin du Gard's conversation and intimate letters has difficulty in seeing what his "other style" may have been; and perhaps he purged his prose too much of its color and flavor. Still, Gallimard's comment would suggest that his simplicity *was* his natural style, and that his matter-of-factness should not be betrayed at the risk of falling into artificiality. In spite of the verve of *Le Père Leleu* and *La Gonfle*, it would seem that for Martin du Gard, character portrayal and analysis and the narration of a serious action belonged in a careful, disciplined prose which would not risk overwhelming the content or falsifying a feeling, a sentiment, a perception. In this view, Martin du Gard is in the best classical French tradition. "La vraie éloquence," wrote Pascal, "se moque de l'éloquence." Not belonging to the category of the greatest writers, for whom accuracy of expression and great force and beauty of language are twins, Martin du Gard nevertheless deserves consideration as one who made language fit the meaning.

Another classical value which Martin du Gard retains is the emphasis on clarity, not just clarity of style but clarity of vision and understanding. In a century when the novel, like poetry, is increasingly used to explore the shadows of man's psyche, of the phenomenon of language itself, and of the human situation—when one demands *resistance* from a work rather than the yielding up of a secret—Martin du Gard's aims remained the traditional ones of clarity of expression and view. He wanted to look carefully enough at the human enigma to say something toward the elucidation, rather than the mere recognition, of it. This is, if not an idealistic viewpoint, at least a somewhat optimistic one. Rather than calling into question the very act of writing, as Mallarmé had done before him and Samuel Beckett, Valéry, and Alain Robbe-Grillet would variously do later, he accepted the assumptions of the French literary tradition and, in particular, of the nineteenth century. Literature is to show and do something. He expressed in his Nobel Prize speech the hope that his portrait of Europe before 1914 might contribute to building European peace.[3] Those who have called him a thorough-going pessimist[4] might recognize that he retained, in the midst of social upheaval and with his keen observation for the destructive currents in man's mind, an understanding of both man and language as possibility.

Clarity was not simplistic for him, however: in *Les Thibault* one finds continual rectifications and cross-reflections of the truth, and, in an effort to corner the truth and capture some understanding, both Antoine's and Jacques' minds return over and over like restless animals to the problems of self and society and morality which gnaw at them. Finally, the effort of the individual is unsuccessful: Antoine recognizes that the puzzle of life is no smaller as he looks at it from the far end; and Armand, in *Un Taciturne*, reminds us that understanding is rare, and that, if it comes, it comes too late. The effort of the novelist, however, is different: escaping from the solipsistic enigma, he can at least see relationships between men and men, and men and their society and their wars. In his microcosmic society he reveals the force of ideas, the tenacious mystery of the passions, the movement of men in time; and he even throws some light on that experience of death which remained for him the most resistant, as the most terrifying, of human experiences.

Clarity thus has a moral and metaphysical value as well as an esthetic one. For the artist, it is the means by which he sees and expresses the tragic quality which is the subject of his writing. For the individual, it is his own elucidation of man's dilemma. Though Antoine cannot, with all his medical knowledge, slow down significantly his decline toward death, he does not cease postulating the value of understanding. He wants to *see* himself die and thus know himself in that supreme way. Thus, he supposes, he may be able to come to terms with himself in the world which, for Martin du Gard no less than for Camus, is the world of the absurd. For society, clarity is a necessary first step. Jacques' futile gesture was based on correct premises: one must get the truth to the masses before they will be other than willing accomplices in their own destruction. Perhaps man cannot organize society successfully—Antoine thinks it will be thousands of years before it *may* happen—but in any case he cannot do so before he knows himself. A conscious life, and a conscious death—these are the *one* moral principle which Antoine recognizes for himself. Thus, the literature of the self, in the individualistic tradition to which Martin du Gard belongs—writing of and for himself—meets the literature of the collectivity in the need for knowledge, and Martin du Gard's illumination of the individual drama can take its place against the background of the contemporary tragic sentiment and the awareness of the world drama, of which, like the figures in Greek tragedy, our individual destinies are a paradigm.

The repeated failures at the end of Martin du Gard's works—the inevitable confrontation of anticipations and realities, of construction and destruction—place the author in the naturalistic tradition, with its social and moral pessimism, and also relate him to the novelists of the absurd of the '30s and '40s. The gloominess of destiny, seen in the careers of André Mazarelles, Jean Barois, and the Thibaults and Fontanins, recalls the accusations that Hardy made of determinism, where men appear as flies to the gods. In a later generation, Camus, who spoke in *The Myth of Sisyphus* of the "bloody mathematics of our condition," nevertheless voiced the more modern view that because life has no transcendent meaning, no universal guarantee, does not mean that it is not worth living. The political action of Luce, Barois, and Jacques is not, in the author's eyes, without resonance on the practical plane. Moreover, the conscious death of Luce and the intensity of experience which is characteristic of Jacques, while not justifying their disappointments and Jacques' absurd early death, nevertheless give to their destinies that quality of "revolt without resignation" which is the stance of the existentialist hero. In spite of the robust humor which characterizes his peasant farces, Martin du Gard is most closely attuned not to a literary tradition that reflects a stable society and widely accepted values, but to the contemporary novel which, to use Gide's phrase, is perpetual questioning. From the interrogation, which calls into question all of modern liberalism, emerge nevertheless the value of life and the value of consciousness, limited but fundamental assumptions which are the point of departure for rethinking man and the world.

Notes and References

Chapter One

1. René Lalou, "Roger Martin du Gard," *Revue de Parie*, 65ᵉ an. (October, 1958), 63-64. The translations of this and subsequent quotations are my own.

2. *Descriptions critiques* (Paris, 1949), I, 61.

3. *La Condition humaine* (Paris, 1946), p. 226.

4. Georg Lukács, *Realism in Our Time*, preface by George Steiner, trans. J. and N. Mander (New York, 1964), pp. 55-59.

5. *A la Recherche du temps perdu*, (Paris, 1954), III, 895.

6. J.-J. Thierry, "Cette gloire paresseuse," *Nouvelle Revue Française*, 6ᵉ an., No. 72 (December, 1958), 1014. See also Martin du Gard, *Œuvres complètes* (Paris, 1955), I, cxxviii. Subsequent references in the text will be to this standard edition of Martin du Gard's works.

7. II, 1107; Roger Froment, "Roger Martin du Gard: Sa mort," *Nouvelle Revue Française*, 6ᵉ an., No. 72 (December, 1958), 965.

8. See *Le Figaro littéraire*, August 30, 1958, and Robert Gibson, *Roger Martin du Gard* (New York, 1961), pp. 12-13.

9. Lalou, p. 64. Extracts from the correspondence appear in Réjean Robidoux, *Roger Martin du Gard et la religion* (Paris, 1964). Other letters, edited by Pierre Herbart, are supposed to be forthcoming. For photographs, reminiscences, and other data see the abundant materials in the "Hommages à Roger Martin du Gard" issue of the *Nouvelle Revue Française*, 6ᵉ an., N. 72 (December, 1958).

10. "Journal d'un écrivain," *La Table ronde*, No. 130 (October, 1958), 175-76.

11. *Descriptions critiques*, pp. 57-58.

12. Lukács affirms that he could not go beyond the bourgeois point of view, ultimately (pp. 96-98).

13. See "Chronologie" and "Souvenirs" in *Œuvres complètes*, I, and *Noizemont-les-Vierges* (Liége, 1928).

14. Paris, 1899. Hébert has an extensive bibliography dealing with questions of religion. Martin du Gard read some of these texts (Robidoux, p. 62) and must have been familiar with many of them.

15. See Chronology above and the Pléiade bibliography for dates of publication.

16. See the Pléiade "Chronologie" and II, 1379, 1381, 1391.

17. Jean Delay, "Commencements d'une amitié," *Nouvelle Revue Française*, 6e an., No. 72 (December, 1958), 979.

18. Extracts appear in the first volume of the *Œuvres complètes*.

19. Delay, p. 983. In 1938, however, Gide wrote in his *Journal* (Paris, 1948), "We're constantly of the same opinion" (p. 1329).

20. See Gide, p. 795. On Martin du Gard's letters to Gide, see Delay, p. 984. See also the *Journal* of Julien Green, I, 1928-34 (Paris, 1938) for portraits of these two men of letters.

21. See Froment, 965-72.

Chapter Two

1. "Portrait et situation de Roger Martin du Gard," *Mercure de France*, No. 1141 (September, 1958), 16.

2. Paris, 1910. See C. D. Boak, "An Early Work by Roger Martin du Gard," *Journal of the Australasian Universities Lang. and Lit. Ass'n*, No. 20 (November, 1963), 318-30.

3. Boak, p. 326.

4. Boak, p. 328.

5. Maurois finds the novel to be an accusation against the bourgeoisie (André Maurois, *Etudes littéraires* [Paris, 1947], II, 166). But André is not a hero, not just a self-portrait (p. 165). He is viewed quite as critically as the bourgeoisie.

Chapter Three

1. *"Jean Barois* et nous," *Nouvelle Revue Française*, 6e an., No. 72 (December, 1958), 1064-67.

2. Gibson traces (p. 44) the occurences of dialogue-fiction in the latter nineteenth century.

3. Roger Martin du Gard "Consultation littéraire: Lettres à Pierre Margaritis," *Nouvelle Revue Française*, 6e an., No. 72 (December, 1958), 1129-33.

4. See I, lxii-lxiii and Chapter 4 below for the reasons which led Martin du Gard to abandon the dialogue form.

5. In *Souvenirs* (I, liv) he recognizes the obsession that the theme of aging and death always had for him. He shows what is nearly a Greek sensitivity to the human destiny and its law of death, which he does not see in Christian terms but rather as the tragic termination of human possibility. By his understanding of aging he makes us think of the Proust of *Le Temps retrouvé*, without the illumination of the narrator. By his vision of man in function of his death as well as his life, he points to Heidegger, Malraux, and Sartre.

6. See Gibson, p, 108, and *Noizemont-les-Vierges* on his early awareness of death.

7. Gibson, p. 33.

8. In *Souvenirs* (I, l-li) Martin du Gard remarks on his indifference to the Dreyfus Affair at the time of the deportation, when he was thirteen. But he notes that he was to attach later "primary importance, for the understanding of my times," to the Affair.

9. See Cécile Delhorbe, *L'Affaire Dreyfus et les écrivains français* (Paris, 1932). Proust's *Jean Santeuil* brings the reader close to the Affair but in an episodic fashion.

10. *Le Roman français depuis Marcel Proust* (Paris, [1932]), p. 162.

11. "Consultation littéraire," pp. 1123, 1126.

12. "Journal d'un écrivain," p. 175.

13. "Consultation littéraire," pp. 1118, 1120, 1122, 1127.

14. See his judgment on books that are useful for only a short time (II, 1396).

15. He speaks of "the necessity of evil in this world, which He created for our best interests"; this argument recalls *Candide*.

16. Charles Moeller, *Littérature du XXe siècle et christianisme* (Tournai, 1962), II, 239.

17. See Henri Clouard, *Histoire de la littérature française du symbolisme jusqu'à nos jours* (Paris, 1949), II, 400-405; Claude-Edmonde Magny, *Histoire du roman français depuis 1918* (Paris, 1950), I, 309-14; and T. W. Hall, "A Note on the So-Called 'Change in Technique' in *Les Thibault* of Roger Martin du Gard," *French Review*, XXVII, No. 2 (December, 1963), 108-13.

18. *The Proud Tower: A Portrait of the World Before the War, 1890-1914* (New York, 1966).

19. See my *Malraux, Sartre, and Aragon As Political Novelists* (Gainesville, 1965).

20. In the latter volumes of *A la Recherche du temps perdu*, for instance, Proust shows the effect of the war on those around him, and thus creates his own type of relativity in historical narration. The war does not exist as an entity; it is, rather, its reflection and its effects. Martin du Gard's presentation of the Dreyfus case has some of the same merits, with less breadth but more intensity.

21. See Tuchman, chapter 4; Guy Chapman, *The Dreyfus Case, A Reassessment* (New York, 1955); Jacques Chastenet, *Histoire de la Troisième République*, III: *La République triomphante, 1893-1905* (Paris, 1955); Nicolas Halasz, *Captain Dreyfus: The Story of A Mass Hysteria* (New York, 1955).

22. Tuchman, pp. 92-93.

23. Maurois (p. 173) suggests Jaurès as a model.

24. Lazare claimed incorrectly that the office boy story was just a front or a frame-up, whereas the charwoman really did find the *bordereau* in a wastebasket (I, 358). The attribution of the *bordereau* to a counterfeiter is false, since Esterhazy wrote it for his own ends.

25. Lazare's text contains a confusion between various forgeries concerning "D" and "P" and "cet animal de Dreyfus," which were not distinguished until later in the Affair (see I, clxviii), and this confusion is kept in *Jean Barois*.

26. See Wayne Booth, *The Rhetoric of Fiction* (Chicago, 1961) on the problem of authorial voice—especially chapters 7 and 10.

27. Robidoux points out how strongly Martin du Gard felt that religion was appropriate for the weak and the dependent, particularly women (pp. 57, 64-65). When Jean returns to Cécile, this association is brought out, as it was in the early parts of the novel.

28. See Micheline Tison-Braun, *La Crise de l'humanisme: Le Conflit de l'individu et de la société dans la littérature française moderne,* I, 1890-1914 (Paris, 1958), p. 398.

29. Quoted in Robidoux, p. 19.

30. Quoted in Robidoux, p. 25. See also p. 46 and Gide, *Journal,* p. 831.

31. Moeller, pp. 238-40, 271.

32. "Projets de préface à *Jean Barois,*" *Nouvelle Revue Française,* 7ᵉ an., No. 84 (December, 1959), 1125.

33. Pp. 1123-24, 1128. Robidoux has examined thoroughly Martin du Gard's departure from the Church and lack of belief, and the light they throw on his work.

Chapter Four

1. "Consultation littéraire: Lettres à Pierre Margaritis," p. 1118.

2. P. 167.

3. See note 17, chapter 3.

4. *The Craft of Fiction* (New York, 1958), chapters 5 and 8.

5. Maurois, p. 179.

6. P. 178.

7. "Point of View in Fiction: The Development of a Critical Concept," *PMLA,* LXX, No. 5 (December, 1955).

8. John Charpentier, "Roger Martin du Gard," *Mercure de France* CCXXV, No. 782 (January 15, 1931), 334, 336.

9. *Journal,* p. 831.

10. *Journal,* p. 1259. Gide also felt that Martin du Gard, while having the instinct of a historian, did not have that of a naturalist, i.e., was a poor observer, seeing what he wanted to see, neglecting the curious species (p. 1146).

11. Gibson, p. 71.
12. Gibson has calculated 1904 (p. 79).
13. Martin du Gard calls Gregory *pasteur* throughout the novel. Since the term pastor was no longer formally used by Christian Scientists after the beginning of the century, this is a misuse of the term. I shall retain it, however, in discussing the episodes where Gregory appears.
14. *The Novel of Adolescence in France* (New York, 1937), p. 164.
15. See Roy, pp. 60, 63.
16. P. 63.
17. P. 71.

Chapter Five

1. Yvonne Davet, *Autour des Nourritures terrestres* (Paris, 1948), p. 166.
2. In *Situations II* (Paris, 1948) Sartre notes that Martin du Gard shows, in this episode, his understanding of the relationship between literature and its audience: *Les Nourritures terrestres* is directed toward "the young reader of the well-off bourgeoisie who is threatened by no exterior peril; who is white; where the ideology of his class is just beginning to decline; who is cultivated" (p. 120). This is precisely the situation of Daniel.
3. See chronological indications, I, 1093-94.
4. These roses will be mentioned again in *La Sorellina*.

Chapter Six

1. Proust does the same thing in the latter volumes of *A la Recherche du temps perdu*, and Gide also, in novels like *L'Immoraliste* and *La Porte étroite*.
2. See Robidoux for interpretation and qualification of Martin du Gard's early statements on his religious development.
3. Unlike Gide in *Les Nouvelles Nourritures*, he refuses to call God that which he cannot understand (I, 1390).

Chapter Seven

1. See note 17, chapter 3. See also Martin Turnell, *The Art of French Fiction* (London, 1959), p. 294.
2. Quoted in Tuchman, p. 96.
3. P. 10.
4. Martin du Gard told René Lalou that this was not a personal confession. He left the Church without a crisis and he did not have these political feelings (pp. 62-63).
5. See I, xiv.

6. Arland, "Chronique des romans," *Nouvelle Revue Française,* 21e an., No. 237 (June, 1933), 986.

Chapter Eight

1. *Collected Poems* (New York, n.d.), p. 175.

Chapter Nine

1. The five works discussed in this chapter will be taken up in the order in which they appear in the *Œuvres complètes.*

2. Schlumberger, "*Vieille France* et l'art," *Nouvelle Revue Française,* 6e an., No. 72 (December, 1958), 1063.

3. Arland, "Chronique des romans," *Nouvelle Revue Française,* 21e an., Nos. 236, 237 (May, June, 1933), 824-26, 985-86.

4. See Gibson, pp. 96-97.

5. *Le Théâtre de Maurice Boissard,* 1907-1923 (Paris, 1943), II, 323.

6. Picon, p. 16.

Chapter Ten

1. "Discours de Stockholm," *Nouvelle Revue Française,* 7e an., No. 77 (May, 1959), 958.

2. *Malraux par lui-même,* ed. Gaëtan Picon (Paris, 1953), p. 66.

3. P. 960.

4. Gibson, p. 115.

Selected Bibliography

PRIMARY SOURCES

Since the individual volumes and several major articles have, with certain exceptions, been assembled in the edition of the complete works, the most easily available, the first publications are not listed here. See Chronology and text for original dates of publication. The *Œuvres complètes* appeared in 1955 in two volumes, with a preface by Albert Camus, in the "Bibliothèque de la Pléiade" (Paris: Gallimard). Letters and fragments are contained in the "Hommage" volumes and others listed under secondary sources. Among other publications by Martin du Gard the following are of interest (see Brenner's book for complete list):

"Le Vieux Colombier," *Nouvelle Revue Française*, 6e an. (December, 1919).

Letter in Marcel Arland, "Chronique des romans," *Nouvelle Revue Française*, 21e an., No. 237 (June, 1933), 985-86.

"Discours de Stockholm," *Nouvelle Revue Française*, 7e an., No. 77 (May, 1959), 956-60.

"Projets de préface à *Jean Barois*," *Nouvelle Revue Française*, 7e an., No. 84 (December, 1959), 1123-28.

Letters to Florent Margaritis, *Cahiers du Sud*, No. 349 (January, 1959).

Works not contained in the *Œuvres complètes*

L'Une de nous. Paris: Grasset, 1910.
Noizemont-les-Vierges. Liége: La Lampe d'Aladin, 1928.
Dialogue. Paris: La Collection blanche, No. 16, 1930.
Correspondence between André Gide and Roger Martin du Gard, Gallimard, Paris, 1967.

Translations

Jean Barois. Trans. STUART GILBERT. New York: Viking, 1949.
The Postman. Trans. JOHN RUSSELL. New York: Viking, 1955.

Recollections of André Gide. Trans. JOHN RUSSELL. New York: Viking, 1953.

Summer 1914. Trans. STUART GILBERT. New York: Viking, 1941.

The Thibaults. Trans. STUART GILBERT. New York: Viking, 1939.

SECONDARY SOURCES

Books on Martin du Gard

ALMÉRAS, GILBERTE. *La Médecine dans Les Thibault de Roger Martin du Gard.* Paris: P. Fournié, 1946. A thorough study of this important aspect of his fiction.

BOAK, DENIS. *Roger Martin du Gard.* Oxford: Clarendon Press, 1963. A systematic study of the man and his works. Sympathetic treatment, and the most comprehensive in English. Detailed bibliography of critical readings.

BORGAL, CLÉMENT. *Roger Martin du Gard.* Paris: Editions universitaires, 1957. In the collection *Classiques du XXe siècle,* this short study is a good introduction to the man and his works.

BRENNER, JACQUES. *Martin du Gard.* Paris: Gallinard, 1961. In the collection *La Bibliothèque idéale.* This is an examination of the man, his friendships, and his works. Good bibliography and iconography. Numerous photographs. Summaries of the works, and selection of significant quotations from them.

DAIX, PIERRE. *Réflexions sur la méthode de Roger Martin du Gard, suivi de Lettre à Maurice Nadeau et autres essais.* Paris: Les Editeurs français réunis, 1957. A seventy-page essay by a novelist, himself author of social and political novels, who deals with Martin du Gard in his relationship to current questions of democracy and socialism.

DESCLOUX, ARMAND. *Psychanalyse du Docteur Thibault de Roger Martin du Gard.* Paris: Editions universitaires, 1965. Thesis by an M. D.

Figaro littéraire. "Hommage à l'écrivain des *Thibault.*" August 30, 1958. Details on his last years and his death. Contains photographs and homage articles by Camus, Mauriac, Duhamel, and others.

GIBSON, ROBERT. *Roger Martin du Gard.* New York: Hillary House, 1961. A too-concise assessment of Martin du Gard's achievement, with good insights.

LALOU, RENÉ. *Roger Martin du Gard.* Paris Gallimard, 1937. A thirty-page monograph, the first to appear, for which the author interviewed Martin du Gard. Appeared in article form in the *Revue de Paris,* August 15, 1937.

Lettres nouvelles. November, 1958. Contains letters from Martin du Gard to a number of correspondents and articles on him.

Selected Bibliography

Livres de France. January, 1960. Letters from Martin du Gard, bibliography, and homage texts by Jean Schlumberger and others.

Nouvelle Revue Française. "Hommage à Roger Martin du Gard." Contains photographs, drawings, reproductions of letters, and articles by a host of major critics and writers. Some unpublished correspondence.

RICE, HOWARD C. *Roger Martin du Gard and the World of the Thibaults.* New York: Viking, 1941. The second study devoted entirely to Martin du Gard, the first in English. Not as satisfactory as later studies.

ROBIDOUX, RÉJEAN. *Roger Martin du Gard et la religion.* Paris: Aubier, 1964. A thorough and sympathetic study of religion in the author's life and works. Contains extracts from many important unpublished letters, including those to Hébert. His intellectual evolution is illuminated by this study.

SCHLOBACH, JOCHEN, *Geschichte und Fiktion in L'Eté 1914 von Roger Martin du Gard,* Wilhelm Fink Verlag, München, 1965.

A number of theses have been devoted in America and France to study of particular aspects of his work. See *Dissertation Abstracts* for individual titles of American studies. In 1964 Nadine D. Savage defended at the Sorbonne a thesis on "L'Influence de Tolstoï dans l'œuvre de Roger Martin du Gard."

Other Critical Works

BRODIN, P.-J. *Les Ecrivains français de l'entre-deux-guerres.* Montreal: Bernard Valiquette, 1942. Places Martin du Gard in his generation.

BROMBERT, VICTOR. *The Intellectual Hero: Studies in the French Novel,* 1880-1955. Chicago: Phoenix Books, 1960. Excellent chapter on *Jean Barois;* studies structure and history in the novel and interprets it as a novel of ideas.

GIDE, ANDRÉ. *Journal des Faux-Monnayeurs,* in *Œuvres complètes,* Vol. XIII. Paris: Nouvelle Revue Française, 1932-39. Allusions to the esthetic discussions between Gide and Martin du Gard in the '20s.

———. *Journal 1889-1939.* "Bibliothèque de la Pléiade." Paris: Gallimard, 1948. With index for all mentions of Martin du Gard, this is a mirror of the friendship between the two writers and their discussions on the novel.

LAPRADE, MICHEL. *Réflexions sur quatre médecins de roman: Essai de définition d'un humanisme médical contemporain.* Bordeaux: Samie, 1948. Study of Antoine Thibault.

LUKÁCS, GEORG. *Realism in Our Time.* Preface by GEORGE STEINER. Trans. K. and N. MANDER. New York: Harper and Row, 1964.

A Marxist study of realism in the European novel since the nineteenth century. Places Martin du Gard in this social realist perspective.

MAGNY, CLAUDE-EDMONDE. *Histoire du roman français depuis 1918.* Vol. I. Paris: Seuil, 1950. This work by a superior analyst contains a long chapter on Martin du Gard which stresses the somber qualities of Martin du Gard's fiction, though paying homage to its power.

MOELLER, CHARLES. *Littérature du XXe siècle et christianisme.* Vol. II. Paris: Casterman, 1953. Written by a sympathetic Catholic, this study focuses on the depiction of religion in *Jean Barois* and tries to show that Martin du Gard was writing in good faith.

PÉGUY, CHARLES. *Notre Jeunesse.* Paris: Gallimard, 1933. The period of the Affaire Dreyfus as lived by the idealistic socialist.

PEYRE, HENRI. The *Contemporary French Novel.* New York: Oxford, 1955. In his short study Peyre places Martin du Gard in the nineteenth and twentieth century French tradition and praises him for his traditional qualities. He lists *Jean Barois* as one of the most significant novels of 1910-30.

ROUSSEAUX, ANDRÉ. *Littérature du XXe siècle.* Vols. I & VI. Paris: Albin Michel, 1938-53. Composed about 1937, one of these essays places Martin du Gard in the fictional tradition and insists upon his nostalgia for Christian belief.

ROY, CLAUDE. *Descriptions critiques.* Vol. I. Paris: Gallimard, 1949. A long and distinguished essay which treats Martin du Gard as a major novelist of ideas, portrayer of society, and creator.

TISON-BRAUN, MADELEINE. *La Crise de l'humanisme; le conflit de l'individu et de la société dans la littérature française moderne.* Vol. I, 1890-1914. Paris: Nizet, 1958. Lengthy study of various moral features of French society at the time when his novels are set.

Articles

BERL, EMMANUEL. "Journal d'un écrivain," *La Table Ronde,* No. 130 (October, 1958, 173-76. Homage to the character and the influence of Martin du Gard on a well-known writer.

BOAK, C. D. "An Early Work by Roger Martin du Gard," *Journal of the Australasian Universities Lang. and Lit. Ass'n,* No. 20 (November, 1963), 318-30. Analysis of *L'Une de nous.*

BRASILLACH, ROBERT. "L'Eté 1914," *L'Action française,* February 4, 1937. Review by the well-known pro-Fascist writer.

Selected Bibliography

CAMUS, ALBERT. "Roger Martin du Gard," *Nouvelle Revue Française*, 3e an., No. 34 (October, 1955), 641-71. This is the same text as Camus' introduction to the *Œuvres complètes*.

CHARPENTIER, JOHN. "Roger Martin du Gard," *Mercure de France*, CCXXV, No. 782 (January 15, 1931), 333-37. An early judgment, highly favorable, on Martin du Gard as a realistic novelist.

HALE, ORON J. "Europe 1914: Was it Morning Light, High Noon, or Twilight?" *Virginia Quarterly Review*, XLI, No. 3 (Summer, 1965), 358-69. His thesis that the war was caused by politicians and diplomats sheds light on Martin du Gard's interpretations.

HALL, THOMAS WHITE. "A Note on the So-Called 'Change in Technique' in *Les Thibault* of Roger Martin du Gard," *French Review*, XXVII, No. 2 (December, 1963), 108-13. Refutes Magny's contention that the structural rupture in *L'Eté 1914* is a serious flaw.

HÉBER-SUFFRIN, "Roger Martin du Gard," *La Grive*, No. 11 (October-December, 1958). Contains quotations from Martin du Gard concerning the war situations in 1914 and 1939 and his attitude on changing politics.

LALOU, RENÉ. "Roger Martin du Gard," *Revue de Paris*, 65e an., (October, 1958), 60-64. Lalou's estimate of Martin du Gard is high. Here, he concentrates on the man.

O'NAN, MARTHA. "Form in the Novel: André Gide and Roger Martin du Gard," *Symposium*, XII, Nos. 1-2 (Spring-Fall, 1958), 81-93. Various structural conceptions applied to novels of Gide and Martin du Gard.

PICON, GAETAN. "Portrait et situation de Roger Martin du Gard," *Mercure de France*, No. 1141 (September, 1958), 5-25. One of the articles written at his death, this assesses sympathetically the man and praises his major works.

ROUDIEZ, LÉON S. "Irony in Roger Martin du Gard," *Romanic Review*, XLVIII, No. 4 (December, 1957), 275-86. Praising *L'Eté 1914* and comparing Martin du Gard's characters favorably to those of Louis Aragon, Roudiez shows that Martin du Gard was most cruel with his ironies toward the characters he liked the best.

WOOD, JOHN S. "Roger Martin du Gard," *French Studies*, XIV, No. 2 (April, 1960), 129-40. On the contemporary qualities of *Les Thibault*. He insists on the optimism of the *Epilogue*.

Index

Index